C000274056

PSL Book of Model Railway Track Plans

PSL Book of Model Railway Track Plans

C.J. Freezer

Patrick Stephens

This book is dedicated to the surgeons and staff of Harefield Hospital, whose skill, dedication, care and concern during August 1986 made the production of this book a pleasure rather than a chore.

© Cyril Freezer, 1988

All rights reserved. No part of this publication may be reproduced, stored in a retrieval system or transmitted, in any form or by any means, electronic, mechanical, photocopying, recording or otherwise, without prior permission in writing from Patrick Stephens Ltd.

First published in 1988

British Library Cataloguing in Publication Data

Freezer, C.J.
    PSL book of model railway track plans.
    1. Railroads — Models
    I. Title
    625.1'9   TF197

    ISBN 0–85059—905–9

Patrick Stephens is part of the Thorsons Publishing Group, Wellingborough, Northamptonshire, NN8 2RQ, England.

Printed and bound in Great Britain by Butler & Tanner Limited, Frome, Somerset.

Contents

Introduction

How wrong can one get? When it was suggested I should produce this book, my first thought was that it was going to be hard going thinking of 70 different layout designs inside a year, let alone drawing them. After all, in the past I'd never produced more than 16 plans in a year. As it turned out, once I got into the swing not only did the plans roll off as though on a production line, but fresh ideas also came flooding in. As the watchmaker's apprentice discovered, there were nearly enough left over for another!

At the outset it was agreed that all plans should be drawn and reproduced to the same scale, so that comparisons were easier. I also decided that they should all fit into a standard home, rather than one provided with a site large enough to accommodate an ideal scheme. With this in mind, most have been drawn to fit sites in houses in which I have lived. The various designs are grouped under specific headings and, with a few exceptions, are angled at the more serious worker who wishes to create a realistic picture of a full-sized railway.

All plans are for indoor layouts, and while they could be shifted out of doors, the whole business of garden layouts requires a special approach, based on the fact that although there is plenty of room, one simply does not fill up the entire area with tracks as one naturally does in the much smaller spaces inside the home.

Whilst you can flip through the book to find a plan that takes your fancy or fits your space, I do ask you to read through from start to finish since not only may you find the treatment of one corner of another plan very much to your liking, but in various places the text also mentions the implicit limitations of a model railway.

It is very easy to draw up an ideal specification for a layout on paper. It is a lot harder putting it into practice. A practical design is always something of a compromise, even though advertising agencies often imply the exact opposite. There are limitations; space is one, but a less obvious one is the size of the human body — some layout designs I've seen seem to have been designed for individuals with a two-metre reach! Most of us realize that money, or to be more precise, the lack of it, also sets limits, but rarely is it added that individual ability and the amount of spare time the enthusiast has at his disposal also set limits to what can be done. In my opinion there is nothing quite as desolate as a layout that is too large, too elaborate or even too finely specified for its owner to finish. Indeed, some of the larger layouts in this book could be a handful for one individual, though as these also require a number of operators, they are ideally suited for a small syndicate of enthusiasts with differing skills and interests, coupled with mutual respect and companionship.

Gauge

Quite apart from the fact that most beginners become confused when faced by our special brand of 'alphabet soup', the relationship of gauge to track design is very special. I can best illustrate this through the common 16.5 mm gauge, OO or HO. Although there is a considerable difference between an OO and an HO layout, so far as the plan is concerned the two are identical. Indeed, in most cases they will be constructed with the same track components. Only the fact that I regard 'OO/HO' as an utterly abominable term has prevented me using it in the text.

I have concentrated on those gauges which are fairly easily obtained, O,OO (with the EM and P4 off–shoots), HO and N. I have also dealt with narrow gauge, again aligning the plans on the commercially–developed systems. What, you may ask, is the position of the more specialized sizes, 1, S, TT, 2 mm scale and Z? Gauge 1 is a specialists' size, and is largely applied to garden layouts. S has only a handful of devotees, all of whom seem perfectly capable of designing their own layouts, in addition to making practically everything else to go with it. TT is better supported, but here I would suggest following OO plans, merely adjusting track centres to suit. The additional space so gained will be invaluable. So far as track plans are concerned, 2 mm scale is as near to N as makes no odds to allow the plans to be easily translated, whilst the ultra-miniature Z gauge should copy N gauge schemes. I have more to say on conversion and adaptation in the final chapter.

Data

Each description is preceded by data giving, in a standardized format, a number of vital statistics. There is, of course, the name, which often has some association with the design, frequently through an atrocious pun. Others have been selected on a very personal basis and I have little doubt that this will give those who know me a good deal of innocent amusement tying up the allusions.

Then I give the gauge for which the layout was designed, followed by the overall dimensions, in metric units. I have used a 300 mm module for the superimposed grid, so those who prefer imperial standards can take this as 12 in. For further details, see the final chapter. Next we have the minimum radius in millimetres. I've tried, for OO gauge, to maintain a minimum of 600 mm,

but occasionally I have gone to 750 mm, which, for the sort of spaces I have used, is about the largest one can use.

In my opinion, the most important thing to consider on any layout plan is the trains that are to run upon it. The motive power I suggest is that I think most suited for the theme I had in mind, but you are free to differ. The train length is expressed in modern bogie coaches, except where I have deliberately selected a period prototype where coaches would be shorter.

Next we have the area of origin, which in the case of Britain is often brought down to a county, particularly where a prototype station is concerned. These items give some indication of the type of model I had in mind when working out the layout, which is amplified by the brief notes at the end.

I have stated whether small, medium or large radius points are employed, which is of considerable importance on the OO, EM and HO layouts. Again this is something you can change if you like, and I also suggest the alternative gauges I consider suitable. Where the gauge is marked with an asterisk, it indicates that some modification is essential, particularly to the relative size of operating wells. Finally, as I mentioned before, there are some brief notes on the design which are intended as a quick guide. For full details, the text should be consulted.

Prototypes

Several plans are based on actual prototypes. In all but one case I have seen the actual station, and I visited the site of the single exception as a boy. All plans are based on prototype practice, which does provide more flexibility than many writers seem to believe. A few plans deal with overseas railways, and whilst there are less than many would wish, I have to point out that this small offering represents a very great advance on the number of foreign prototypes given in planbooks from other countries — nil!

These plans emphasize features of Continental and USA practice which differ materially from British arrangements. However, there are great similarities since track layouts are determined by the mechanics of rail-borne transport, while the national characteristics are mainly provided by the landscape, buildings and above all the locomotives and rolling stock. The only point to watch with double track layouts is that France and Switzerland join Britain in following left-hand running, but the rest run on the right. Plans for these countries should therefore be arranged as mirror images.

Symbols

All plans use a common set of symbols, most of which have been used to represent railway features for over a century. However, there are some additional refinements, so to avoid confusion I have provided a full key. In addition, the main railway buildings are labelled according to a standard set of abbreviations. Other buildings are left unmarked for although I had a clear pic-ture of what they should be when I was drawing the plan, you are bound to have different ideas.

I have been anything but rigid in my use of screen textures. Here my object has been to differentiate between adjacent areas of landscape rather than to provide an accurate key to land utilization. Again, feel free to disagree. Indeed please do, but read the final chapter first!

Key to abbreviations

C	Coaling stage	SB	Station building
ES	Engine shed	SC	Signal cabin
GF	Ground frame	WK	Railway workshop
GS	Goods shed	WT	Water tank

The symbols

	Track		Point (turnout)
	Track (narrow gauge)		Crossing
	Loops, fiddle yard etc		Double slip
	Hidden track		
	Ash pit/ Inspection pit		Turntable
	Coal drops		
	Coal bins (coal staithes)		Bridge or viaduct
	Backscene		Tunnel
	Wall		
	Fence		Overall roof
	Footbridge		
	Footbridge with goods lift		Yard crane / Water crane
	Barrow crossing		Buildings
	Accommodation crossing		Platelayer's hut
	Road overbridge		Platform
			Goods bank
	Level crossing		Cattle dock
			Baseboard joint
	Slope		Lift-out section
	River		Paved areas
	Canal with lock gate		Garden, shrubs etc
	Water and trees		Rough ground, fields, seashore etc
	Hedgerow		Preferred operation point
	Optional section		
	Filler section		Duck under

CHAPTER 1
A solid start

A model railway is rather a large item, which is hardly surprising when one remembers that the prototype is measured in kilometres. Obviously, a thoroughgoing model of a complete railway is out of the question, so we have to select a small portion on which to concentrate. Even so, a small model railway is larger than the majority of big models in other diciplines. Hence all model railways are a compromise between what is realistically feasible and what we would really like to do. Even the model that faithfully reproduces one single station to exact scale is still a compromise, for the rest of the system has had to be omitted and with it, in many cases, the more fascinating trains that just don't reach the station that has been modelled. Is all the might and majesty of the GWR really represented by a scale model of Ashburton? I think not!

Clearly, even in the smallest practical scales, one would prefer to have a permanent railway room for the layout, but at the outset what one has is usually quite different. A railway room, whilst desirable and, with some forethought and determination, attainable, is mostly a pleasant fantasy. We start on less ambitious lines, and are much the better for the experience, since the man who tries to make the definitive layout at his first attempt rarely, if ever, succeeds.

With the distinction between toy and model blurred beyond easy distinction, the best dividing line is that a model railway is built on a baseboard, is framed by scenery of one sort or another and, most important of all, an attempt is made to simulate reality.

Initial thoughts usually turn to a single solid baseboard. In N gauge this does make good sense, as I shall show later, but for the time being I am only considering OO and HO gauges.

Plan No. 1 Lochaber
OO gauge 1.20 m × 0.90 m; Steam motive power; **Country of origin** Britain; **Other recommended gauges** HO, N; **Minimum radius** 375 mm; **Train length** 2 coaches; Small points; Basic train set oval with one siding and scenic development.

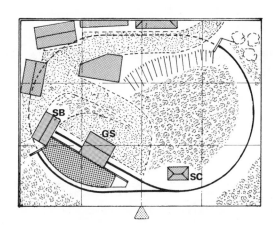

Plan 1   Lochaber

Lochaber is included for sentimental reasons, for I drew it in 1939, my first serious essay into layout design. The idea was to hide the back of the conventional oval of sectional track under a small town, and add a low backscene. I fear that the scenic design owed more to the Home Counties than the Highlands, but I just felt at the time that a line north of the border was more romantic.

It never got built. When Hitler's troops invaded Poland I was evacuated to Weston-super-Mare, where pondering over the plan of the layout during the phoney war, I realized its snags. The siding was so short it could only hold a couple of wagons and operation was clearly limited. Ah well, back to the drawing board! I was wrong. Although limited in operation, **Lochaber** is a useful 'quickie' on which to learn the basics of the hobby. It also has its value as an exhibition filler.

Plan No. 2 Binns Road
OO gauge 1.50 m × 1.35 m; Open motive power; **Country of origin** Britain; **Other recommended gauges** HO, N; **Minimum radius** 375 mm; **Train length** 3 coaches; Small points; Developed train set concept, suitable for sectional track.

Plan No.2 offers more operational promise and by having a lay-by loop behind the backscene it is a little more practical. It is also slightly larger

and is essentially unidirectional, with the trains rotating 'widdershins', that is anti-clockwise. Somehow most of my plans have this bias, probably because I am left-handed.

The scheme was first drawn out for the old Hornby Dublo track system, hence the name, **Binns Road** from their Liverpool address. I have not shown track joints, largely because different sectional track systems have different geometries and, of course, flexible track is a viable alternative if you are not using what you already have to hand. You must use small radius points and it is a lot easier to use sectional curved track than to lay flexible track to such tight curves.

Plan No. 3 Camberwick Green
OO gauge 1.80 m × 1.60 m; Open motive power; **Country of origin** Britain; **Other recommended gauges** HO, N; **Minimum radius** 450 mm; **Train length** 3 coaches; Small points; Double-track oval on 6 ft × 4 ft baseboard, suitable for sectional track.

Following on from this Plan No. 3, **Camberwick Green**, is nothing more or less than a developed train set oval, and is included to ram home a vital point. A baseboard this large, 1.80 × 1.20 m, has to be pushed into a corner in most homes, which means that the back is, to all intents and purposes, inaccessible since the board is as large as a double bed. It could stand free in a medium-

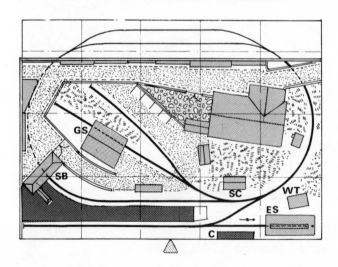

Plan 2   Binns Road

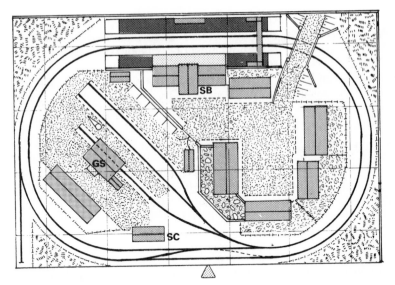

Plan 3   Camberwick
                Green

sized bedroom, but there would be space for little else in the room.

In **Camberwick Green** we have a large town
square which is roughly the size of a hand and is
there to take your weight whilst you scrabble for
those back tracks. Even so, it is not going to be
easy, so I have not set any points on the far side.
Throughout this book, you will find that
wherever the tracks are at extreme reach I have
avoided pointwork to minimize the risk of

derailments. The little spur on the outer circuit is
there to hold a spare locomotive.

This plan is designed to allow you to run two
trains simultaneously, one on each track.
However, the dotted crossover is going to make
this more difficult, since you cannot swap a train
on to a track that is already occupied. It is not
prototypical, so if you want to get away from
merely playing trains, omit it, and save the cost
of a pair of points!

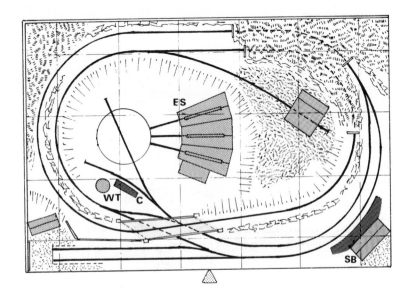

Plan 4   Allentown

Plan No. 4   Allentown

HO gauge 1.80 m × 1.20 m; Steam motive power; **Country of origin** USA c. 1885; **Other recommended gauges** OO, N; **Minimum radius** 375 mm; **Train length** 3 coaches; Small points; 'Looped eight' plan inspired by John Allen's *Gorre & Daphetid.*

We now look at two overseas schemes. **Plan No. 4** is set in the State of Chaos, USA, the place where westerns are set. The design is inspired by John Allen's original Gorre and Daphetid, hence **Allentown**, and is an example of the looped eight design which doubles the trackage in a given area and, by introducing gradients, increases the scenic effect. The two buildings in the corner are the sheriff's office (the Allentown Jail?) and the saloon, which as followers of this genre will know, are the only buildings of note in a western town. It is limited to short trains and in my opinion best set in the nineteenth century, with wood-burning 4-4-0s and short, clerestory–roofed coaches.

Plan No. 5   Fleischmark

HO gauge 2.40 m × 1.20 m; Electric motive power; **Country of origin** Germany; **Other recommended gauges** OO, N; **Minimum radius** 375 mm; **Train length** 5 coaches; Medium points; Continental out-and-back scheme for solid baseboard.

Fleischmark is strictly Continental for it has the ladder tracks and double slips so characteristic of the prototype. It will be seen that the majority of turnouts are within very easy reach of the operating side of the board, and all are open for inspection. With the high and low level stations cheek by jowl in this fashion, one can treat them as one unit scenically whilst enjoying the visual effect of a multi-level scheme. The design gives out-and-back running with a continuous run. The passing loop on the low level main line helps to improve the operating pattern and it would not be too difficult to devise a realistic timetable for this layout. I have suggested electric traction, though the upper yard would probably be best worked by a diesel shunter.

Although slightly larger than the other plans, paradoxically **Fleischmark** is the easiest of all the solid layouts in this chapter to house, since it will fit comfortably across the far end of a garage. All you need to do is to raise it high enough to allow the car bonnet to go underneath and you are

Plan 5   Fleischmark

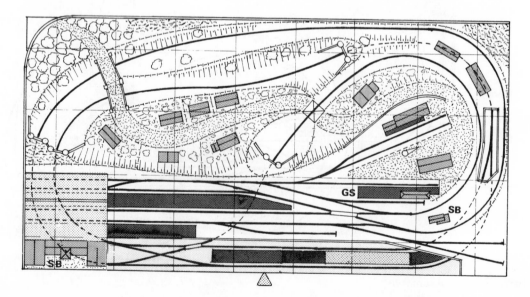

home and dry. However, I would place it some 400 mm away from the rear wall to give access to the far tracks.

Plan No. 6 Zeals

OO gauge 1.80 m × 1.60 m; Steam motive power; **Country of origin** Britain; **Other recommended gauges** HO; **Minimum radius** 450 mm; **Train length** 3 coaches; Medium points; Compact branch layout with central operating well on six baseboards.

The easiest solution to access on this size of layout is shown in Plan No.6, which has a hole in the middle for the operator. Moreover, instead of being built on a single unwieldy board it is carried on six smaller, easily-handled baseboards and so can be dismantled and stored, or taken to an exhibition. I would advise the use of curved points on the main oval, and with about 10 per cent more space, you could use a 600 mm radius

and large radius points throughout, with enormous improvement to both appearance and running.

Zeals introduces the popular branch line theme and so would normally be worked by tank locomotives with, perhaps, an occasional visit from a diesel railcar. The use of an 0-6-0 tender loco for goods would be prototypical, but, with a limited train length, a trifle counter-productive. A small overall roof is shown, and in GW territory one of the Brunel structures is indicated.

The provision of the run-round loop clear of the platform roads allows one to terminate a train in the through platform as well as in the terminal roads proper. However, the optional chain-dotted tracks outside the baseboard proper are a simple fiddle yard which, as I shall explain in the next chapter, is the key to realistic operation in confined spaces.

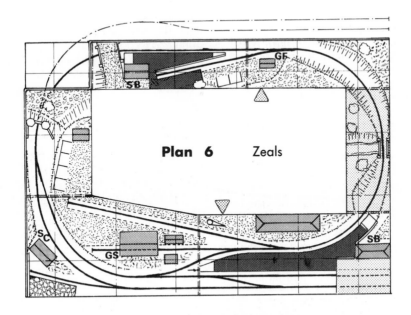

Plan 6   Zeals

CHAPTER 2

A complete fiddle

The development of the fiddle yard has reached the point where few advanced British layouts are without one. The basic concept, a convenient means of reversing trains in a limited area, has been augmented by the realization that a magazine of trains, located off-stage, allows one to operate an authentic schedule following, if desired, the actual working timetable of a selected station. In addition, it provides a very large storage capacity, which in itself is of immense value as your collection of models grows — and grows and grows!

The fiddle yard is where you fiddle with trains, so you can pick up a locomotive and put it on the other end of the train, turning it from end to end if so desired. You can re-arrange the stock, load or unload open wagons; in short, you can do all the things that are not supposed to be done, thus allowing the actions in the visual part of the model to be correct to prototype.

Equally, the whole thing is, in slang parlance, a fiddle. The trains don't go anywhere, they just disappear through a hole in the backscene into an area that, unlike the layout proper, is deemed not to have any 'real' existence. In imagination, that all-important part of our hobby, the trains head off to London or wherever, according to the timetable. In fact, they come to an undignified halt just past the scenic break. Rather than depict fiddle yards in an abstract form, I have chosen to display them as part of simple layouts, not only killing two birds with one stone, but at the same time giving some idea of how they can be arranged.

Plan No. 7 Seaton
OO gauge 3.00 m × 0.30 m; Steam motive power; **Country of origin** Britain; **Other recommended gauges** O, HO, N; **Minimum radius** 1,000 mm; **Train length** 3 coaches; Large points; Branch terminus based on prototype with sector plate fiddle yard.

Plan No. 7 shows the simplest possible system, a

Plan 7   Seaton

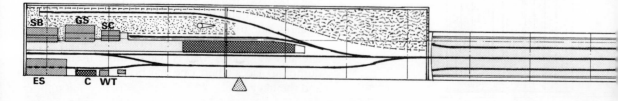

sector plate fiddle yard abutting directly on to the terminus which is a shortened version of the former SR station at **Seaton** in Devon, modelled as one would see it standing on the mud-banks of the River Axe. It has the classic, small, single-track terminus plan, a run-round loop against the main platform and two sidings, one of which doubled as a bay road on summer Saturdays. The design dated from the 'thirties, and when the adjacent holiday camp brought a lot of traffic to the branch the platforms could easily accommodate a ten-coach train.

The fiddle yard consists of three long roads on a swivelling base, which are manually aligned with the exit road. A simple locking device is often employed but this is not absolutely essen-tial as friction holds the table in place well enough. It is necessary to lift locomotives and place them manually on the other end of the train. In this particular setting the trains go straight on to the sector plate without any form of disguise, for the next mile or so of the branch ran on an embankment alongside the Axe, the route taken by the present Seaton Tramway.

Plan No. 8 Elton

OO gauge 2.40 m × 2.10 m; Steam motive power; **Country of origin** Britain; **Other recommended gauges** O, EM, HO, N; **Minimum radius** 600 mm; **Train length** 4 coaches; Medium points; L–shaped layout with screened fiddle yard served by points.

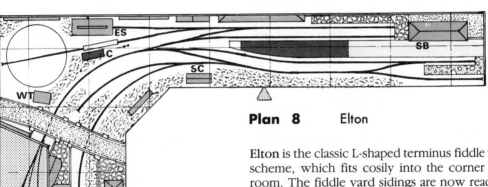

Plan 8   Elton

Elton is the classic L-shaped terminus fiddle yard scheme, which fits cosily into the corner of a room. The fiddle yard sidings are now reached by points, and are hidden behind a low backscene. The entry is disguised by an over-bridge, more probable than a tunnel portal, whilst the goods yard runs in front of the storage roads. This allows room for a thoroughgoing yard, with all the major trimmings and allows for two-operator use of **Elton**, which is often convenient.

The turntable is capable of handling a large locomotive, but the shed is only suited for the smaller branch engine. Note that there is ample space between the end of the goods loading plat-form and the entry point of the locomotive yard to allow one to get to the turntable whilst vans are at the dock. The small spur between the main line and the goods road is one of those useful dumping places where one may hold spare vans and the like.

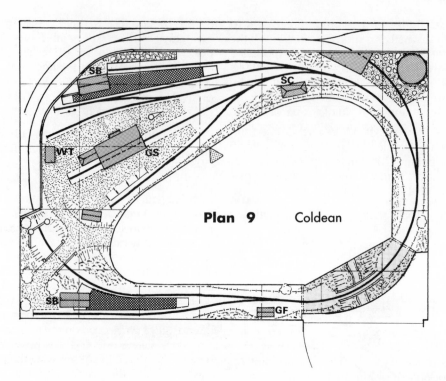

Plan 9   Coldean

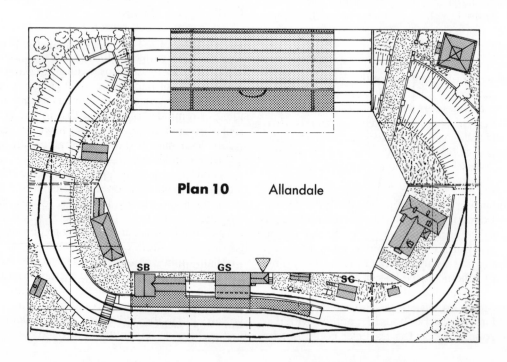

Plan 10   Allandale

Plan No. 9   Coldean

OO gauge 2.05 m × 1.45 m; Steam motive power; **Country of origin** Britain; **Other recommended gauges** O, HO, N*; **Minimum radius** 600 mm; **Train length** 3 coaches; Medium points; Branch terminus featuring Maurice Dean pattern fiddle yard.

This shows the style of fiddle yard devised by my old friend Maurice Dean. Here, the sidings are located behind **Coldean** in a spot convenient to the operator, whilst a spur links them to the main line to give a continuous run. I have shown this as a siding to the gasworks, the track running into one of the buildings and then through the backscene.

The terminus is fairly conventional but cramped, since the layout is designed to fit into a small garden shed. A lift-out section goes across the doorway, and a small halt, with a siding long enough to hold the short trains used on this line, is provided here.

Plan No. 10   Allandale

OO gauge 2.25 m × 1.80 m; Steam motive power; **Country of origin** Britain; **Other recommended gauges** O, HO; **Minimum radius** 450 mm; **Train length** 2 coaches; Medium points; Small through branch station, based on Allan Wright's *Cheviotdale*.

On a continuous run, you can have storage loops to simulate the rest of the railway system, and examples of this arrangement will be shown later in this book. As a fan of points takes up a good deal of space, the sliding magazine is occasionally used instead to save valuable space. This is not too difficult to arrange, as one can mount the sub-base on two lengths of plastic draw slides.

Allandale is a small layout using this type of yard. It will be seen that not only are there a number of locomotive and van spurs at each end of the traverser, but also that the two entry roads do not line up. This arrangement produces a point-to-point scheme at the loss of test run facilities.

I am assuming that, like Alan Wright's Cheviotdale on which it is patterned, **Allandale** would normally be housed entirely within a small room, and so the traverser could not be pushed back beyond the extent of the baseboard. This restriction would not, of course, apply at exhibitions; the baseboard has been shown sectioned to permit removal for this purpose.

Plan No. 11   St Newlyn East

OO gauge 3.00 m × 2.10m; Steam motive power; **Country of origin** Britain; **Other recommended gauges** EM/P4, HO; **Minimum radius** 750 mm; **Train length** 4 coaches; Large points; Turn-of-the-century layout with Denny–style fiddle yard.

Plan No. 11 is one of the more sophisticated layouts in this book, for whilst it is an apparently simple, straightforward scheme, it employs the fiddle yard system developed by Peter Denny. A turntable track is fed through a fan of points. The turntable pivot, plus the table, must be moved back mechanically some 30 to 50 mm to clear the locating pins before the table can be turned end for end. Stops are needed on the turntable to prevent stock falling out, and it is possible to link these so that the action of screwing the pivot forward also lifts the barrier. With a properly-designed timetable, this end-for-end turning need only take place at roughly one hour intervals.

The station, which started out to be a rough copy of the first station at Seaton, acquired lots of extras in the process. **St Newlyn East** is a conventional branch terminus, with a locomotive shed capable of handling a 4-4-0 or 2-6-0, but nothing larger. Once again, there is a gasworks siding, a reminder of the fact that in the great days of steam any medium-sized town had one and the local railway did a good traffic with coal inward and coke and coal tar outward.

A small halt is provided, partly for scenic effect but mainly to allow an operating distinction between local and express trains; the former stop here, the latter do not. The main line radii, whilst still well under-scale, are sufficient to permit the use of EM if desired.

In light outline close to the halt I have sketched a micro-computer. It could merely hold the timetable in data statements, ready to be displayed on the screen. It could control the fiddle yard, just as the fiddle yard on Peter Denny's Buckingham is computer-controlled. As his

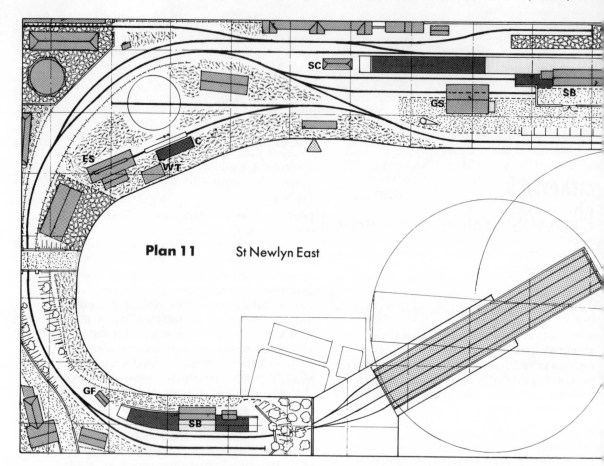

Plan 11   St Newlyn East

computer is a very elementary electro-mechanical device with a punched tape memory, I imagine that a very basic home micro would do the job admirably, providing it is practicable to interface it with the fiddle yard turnouts. As suitable micros are now coming on to the second-hand market this is a wholly practical arrangement – providing you know a good deal about computing, or have an associate who does.

These are just five ways of arranging a fiddle yard. There are other approaches, most of which will turn up throughout this book, but I have said enough to show how the arrangement is employed and basically how it works. It allows a relatively simple layout to be intensively operated with a wide variety of trains, and in the next chapter we will apply this to some compact OO gauge layouts.

CHAPTER 3

How small is too small?

In the first chapter I briefly touched on small sized OO or HO layouts, but with the aid of fiddle yards, there is opportunity for further compression — or is there? In this section I will look at some seemingly plausible schemes for space-saving which don't quite work out, if one is aiming for a layout that will sustain interest after construction. A model railway does, I think, need to have a reasonable operating potential if it is to be worthwhile.

Plan No. 12   Little Appenin
OO gauge 1.20 m × 0.25 m; Steam motive power; **Country of origin** Britain; **Other recommended gauges** O, EM/P4, HO; **Minimum radius** 1,000 mm; **Train length** 2 coaches; Large points; Minimum sized branchline halt, limited operation.

It is as well to be sure that the layout really is small. Plan No. 12 only appears to be compact, for by the time that the two fiddle yards needed to complete **Little Appenin** have been added, it will at the very least be double its length. It is very similar to **Lochaber**, but thanks to the

greater storage capacity of the fiddle yards, it allows one to accommodate more trains.

Little Appenin still has limited operational characteristics, and shows clearly that if you make a model of a station where very little happens on the prototype, very little can happen on the model! If you disagree, build it and see for yourself, as it is a worthwhile exercise. As a first trial of, say, O gauge, **Little Appenin** would be perfect, but it is also equally suited as a way of discovering if you can build really effective scenery. Although this is a very popular theme, one can see at many smaller exhibitions, layouts where the builder has gone to enormous pains to show that he can't model grass and finds it completely impossible to build a tree!

A layout ought to have some operational potential, and reproduce the workings of the prototype, which in the steam age could be quite considerable. Otherwise, it is still only a train set, no matter what scale/gauge combination one employs, or how high the level of craftsmanship involved. After all, you can see train sets in the larger stores with models that would, a few years

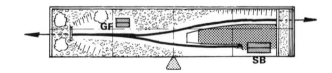

Plan 12   Little Appenin

ago, have been hailed as superb examples of true scale modelling, were they built by amateurs!

It is very easy to overlook the fact that, in the golden days of railways, virtually everything needed by the community was delivered in a four-wheeled wagon of one sort or another, and even a branch line freight train would be twenty wagons or more in length, a contrast with the very short passenger trains. If the fiddle yards were made long enough it would certainly be possible to run ten-wagon trains, but at Little Appenin, you cannot do a lot with them. You can only drop off goods wagons from a left-to-right running freight train, the locomotive is in the wrong place in the reverse direction.

Plan No. 13a   Doxbury

OO gauge 1.80 m × 0.30 m; Steam motive power; **Country of origin** Britain; **Other recommended gauges** O, EM/P4; **Minimum radius** 1,000 mm; **Train length** 2 coaches; Large points; Branch line halt with goods loop.

The next two layouts, Plan No. 13a and Plan No. 13b, are provided with goods loops. These are not, as they might appear, passing loops, but are there to allow freight and mixed trains to drop wagons regardless of the direction of travel. In practice, the wagons would be left on the loop and moved into the end sidings, either by a horse or by two or three strong men.

At **Doxbury** this is fairly obvious, since the goods shed is on the loop, with a short spur feeding the coal yard, which is provided with a small array of coal bins (often referred to as coal staithes). This tiny layout shows the basic elements of a steam-age station, but in place of a full signal cabin we have a ground frame. The distinction is simple enough: **Doxbury** is not a block post, and even though I have shown the frame in a tiny cabin, there would be no block instruments.

Plan No. 13b   Cullitun

OO gauge 1.80 m × 0.30 m; Steam motive power; **Country of origin** Britain; **Other recommended gauges** O, EM/P4, HO; **Minimum radius** 1,000 mm; **Train length** 2 coaches; Large points; Branch line halt with goods loop and two sidings.

Cullitun has the goods shed clear of the loop and the platform to one end. As a result, it could be used as a terminus, but if this were the case, it would help if it were to be extended at least another 300 mm to give a longer platform and a bigger bay road.

This type of station was found on branch lines, and in model form is best employed as a subsidiary feature to larger layouts. Whilst mainly steam age prototypes, some remained to see diesels, when freight trains would be much shorter. Indeed, it is possible to assemble sets of trains for different periods and run them on separate occasions to provide variety, as these stations hardly altered from the 1890s to their demise in the '50s and '60s.

Plan No. 14   Walkley Sidings

OO/HO gauge 1.80 m × 2.80 m; Open motive power; **Country of origin** Britain (Cornwall); **Other recommended gauges** O, EM/P4, HO; **Minimum radius** 1,000 mm; **Train length** 4 wagons; Medium points; Copy of A.R. Walkley's original HO shunting yard.

Shunting can be great fun on these simple layouts, but it is better on a design such as **Walkley Sidings**, a close copy of an HO layout first built over 60 years ago by A.R. Walkley. It is designed to fold in the centre, the hinges being disguised by the lift-off overbridge, producing a compact box which protects the layout whilst stored or in transit. All shunting movements can be carried out within the confines of the baseboard and, although I show a lead-off track which will allow the layout to be incorporated into a larger scheme at some future date, there is no need for a fiddle yard at all. This is the smallest complete OO layout in this book.

This layout, as with all others in this chapter, is an excellent test bed for auto-couplers. Indeed, the original layout demonstrated A.R. Walkley's excellent coupling which, after commercial development, we now know as the 'tension lock' coupling and is the *de facto* standard for British OO gauge ready-to-run stock. Needless to say, you could use any other design of auto-coupling, or even one of your own construction.

Plan 13a
Doxbury

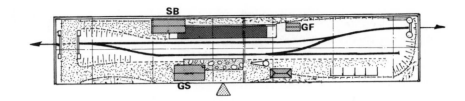

Plan 13b
Cullitun

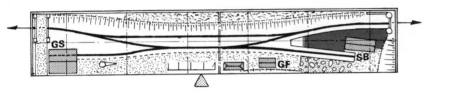

Plan 14
Walkley Sidings

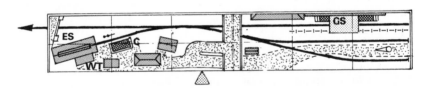

Plan 15   Brill

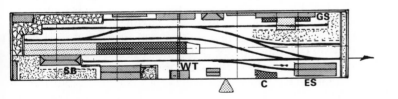

Plan No. 15   Brill

OO gauge 1.65 m × 0.325 m; Steam motive power; **Country of origin** Britain; **Other recommended gauges** O, EM/P4; **Minimum radius** 750 mm; **Train length** 2 coaches; Medium points; Branch terminus on folding baseboards, all shunting within station.

This plan, whilst even shorter, does need a fiddle yard, but as with **Walkley Sidings**, all shunting

movements on **Brill** can be confined to the main baseboards. Again they can fold, but here the hinges are disguised with removable buildings. It is just possible to accommodate a small 4-6-0 and two bogie coaches in the platform which, whilst stretching probability beyond all reasonable bounds, is nevertheless great fun.

Both **Brill** and **Walkley Sidings** depict a landscape-free scenic approach, being framed

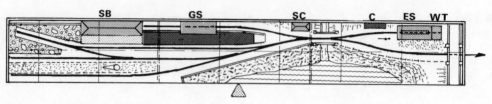

Plan 16   Penhagen

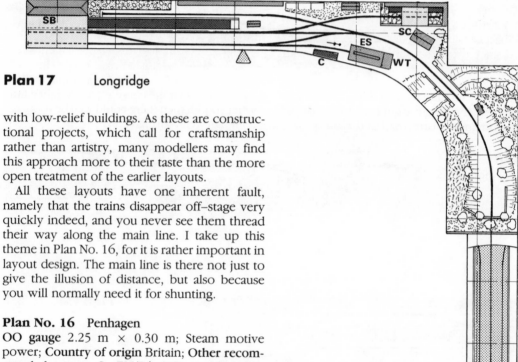

Plan 17   Longridge

with low-relief buildings. As these are constructional projects, which call for craftsmanship rather than artistry, many modellers may find this approach more to their taste than the more open treatment of the earlier layouts.

All these layouts have one inherent fault, namely that the trains disappear off–stage very quickly indeed, and you never see them thread their way along the main line. I take up this theme in Plan No. 16, for it is rather important in layout design. The main line is there not just to give the illusion of distance, but also because you will normally need it for shunting.

Plan No. 16   Penhagen
OO gauge 2.25 m × 0.30 m; Steam motive power; **Country of origin** Britain; **Other recommended gauges** O, EM/P4, HO, N; **Minimum radius** 1,000 mm; **Train length** 3 coaches; Large points; Branch terminus with loco shed extension.

Consider **Penhagen**, a small branch line terminus of the steam age which is accommodated on two relatively short, narrow baseboards. A third baseboard provides a short length of main line and a locomotive depot, which gives some room for shunting in the open. It can be awkward to shunt in the fiddle yard, so it is worth contriving the extra length to accommodate a short section of main line. Indeed, one can have the best of both worlds: a compact station, omitting the main line and engine shed with a shortish fiddle yard for home use, with the option of the extra unit for exhibition use where more room is available. This might require the construction of two fiddle yards, but as sector plates are easy and cheap to make, this is not really a problem. Omitting a section is useful, and, in later plans, a shaded arrow will indicate the optional board.

Plan No. 17 Longridge

OO gauge 2.50 m × 2.00 m; Steam motive power; **Country of origin** Britain; **Other recommended gauges** O, EM/P4, HO, N; **Minimum radius** 600 mm; **Train length** 2 coaches; Medium points; L-pattern branch terminus and fiddle yard.

The trouble with a completely straight arrangement is that it needs a very long wall to accommodate it, so in Plan No. 17 we have a very popular way round this difficulty, the L formation. **Longridge** will fit into a small bedroom, and would be a very handy scheme for a teenage enthusiast since it will not seriously interfere with the room's use as a bedroom-cum-study.

The track plan is fairly conventional, apart from the entry into the factory siding. To avoid a kickback off the single siding, it comes direct from the main platform road and crosses over the siding. This use of a crossing is by no means unusual on the prototype, but it is rare in model form, yet it adds to the visual complexity of the station throat and so makes for a more attractive layout.

The intrusive chimney-breast, often found in small bedrooms, is shown just to prove that it is not necessarily an awkward obstruction. I have introduced some scenery along the short leg of the L, whilst as the entry to the sector plate fiddle yard is by way of a tunnel, I have suggested a fairly elaborate portal. One of the superb Faller 'Loreli' structures would be a lovely finish to the run.

Whilst I have implied this is a permanent structure, it would be useful to break it down into sections. Certainly, the fiddle yard could well be removable, and if the curve were brought a little further round, then there could well be room for a complete train turntable.

CHAPTER 4
Prototype pros and cons

If you have not noticed my references to the importance of following the prototype, do not worry as I shall return to the subject time and time again. If you want a model railway to look and operate as if it were the full-sized original, then you must go back to the real thing and not simply copy someone else's model. Remember, almost every model railway has some element of compromise; the edges are blurred and the more it is copied, the greater the blurring.

There is a danger here, too. Many people are over-emphasizing 'research' to the point where the best excuse for inaction is, 'My research is not yet complete'. For most people research is quite unnecessary, as there are now plenty of books which have exhaustive detail on British prototype practice. I don't say you can find out everything, but you can only run into trouble if you begin by insisting that you are going to model a particularly obscure prototype station.

In the 1950s, research was simple. You simply took the train to your chosen prototype armed with camera, notebook and steel tape, plus plenty of sandwiches and a thermos flask. There you made an on-the-spot survey, went home — and as often as not discovered that you had failed to cover some vital part of the station.

Today, you can buy a book of station layout plans covering 40 or 50 stations for less than it would have cost you to visit one station in the 1950s. So if you want to model an actual prototype these books, supplemented by the ex-

cellent historical monographs on railway byways now so plentiful in specialist bookshops, provide enough information to enable you to make a reasonable model of any suitable station. By this I mean one which has been reasonably well-recorded and which can be fitted into the space you have available. If you select an obscure station, you will probably get nowhere, since even if photographs were taken it is unlikely they are actually available and may even have been lost.

However, it is not necessarily a good idea slavishly to model an actual station, so in this chapter I shall look at the advantages and disadvantages, selecting two prototypes I know well.

Plan No. 18   Ashburton
OO gauge 2.30 m × 0.46 m; Steam motive power; **Country of origin** Britain (Devon); **Other recommended gauges** O, EM/P4, HO, N; **Minimum radius** 1,000 mm; **Train length** 4 coaches; Medium points; Branch terminus based on GWR prototype.

Plan No. 18, my first example, is the ever-popular **Ashburton**, which is featured in Paul Karau's *Great Western Termini* (published by Oxford Publishing Company), and drawings and ample photographs are available. It is fairly small and very simple. It seems obvious that **Ashburton** would be a very straightforward modelling project, particularly as the locomotives and roll-

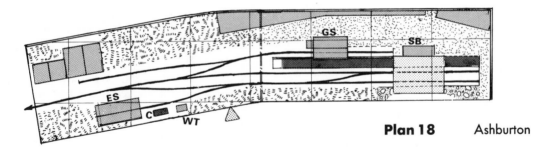

Plan 18   Ashburton

ing stock are available ready-to-run in 4 mm scale and as kits in other sizes.

Unfortunately, **Ashburton** has some severe limitations. For a start, the variety of trains on offer is small, mainly push-pull locals from Totnes, freight, including cattle trains from the town's market, and the occasional through special. Worse is to come. Operationally it's a pig. Whenever, on Ashburton Fair days, cattle traffic became heavy, they not only stopped the passenger trains at Buckfastleigh, but on at least one occasion managed to get two locomotives jammed immovably behind the wagons, a situation which was only got over by bending both the rules and part of the point rodding.

One snag was the kickback siding to the mill. On the prototype, wagons were put in place with the help of a dray horse, an extremely useful shunting device in great demand during the first century of railway development, though a trifle difficult to model effectively. Later, rope shunts were carried out, but these are not really practical in 4 mm scale, though they are possible in 7 mm. To shunt with a locomotive involves clearing part of the goods shed siding. Ugh!

On top of that, Ashburton never had a signal box, although I have it on the authority of the last stationmaster, Dick Dunwoody, that it once had the cast plate for the box. The plate disappeared, I would like to think into a private collection, but more likely it went into a scrap furnace.

Plan No. 19   Chagford
OO gauge 2.30 m × 0.45 m; Steam motive power; **Country of origin** Britain (Devon); **Other recommended gauges** O, EM/P4, HO, N; **Minimum radius** 1,000 mm; **Train length** 4 coaches; Large points; Modification to Ashburton layout.

So, in exactly the same space, we have Plan No. 19, a more convenient scheme with the same number of points. The mill siding has been turned around and the surrounding buildings modified to provide a complete frame for the model. **Chagford** is reminiscent of **Seaton** (Plan No. 7), with the locomotive shed moved and an overall roof added. It is, I feel, a rather better design than **Ashburton** and, since it is not an actual prototype, does not restrict modelling only to trains that ran on the full-sized railway. Not

Plan 19   Chagford

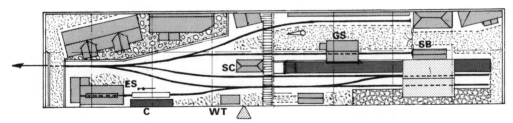

that following a prototype need confine you in this fashion, though if you are going to deviate it seems to me pointless to go to all the trouble of strictly modelling a prototype station in the first instance.

Plan No. 20 St Ives
OO gauge 3.225 m × 1.875 m; Steam motive power; **Country of origin** Britain (Cornwall); **Other recommended gauges** EM, HO, N; **Minimum radius** 600 mm; **Train length** 4 coaches; Medium points; Cornish branch terminus based on prototype.

As this plan clearly shows, **St Ives** in Cornwall was a superb prototype. I thought so when I first saw an aerial photograph, my wife said as much when first she saw it on holiday. It lay in a wide sweep around the bay, with a scenic division into three levels, beach, railway and town, which makes for an attractive model. The layout, whilst simple, is adequate to sustain interest in operation. It is worth noting that the release crossover is well up the platform, while in practice the roads beyond made very convenient carriage sidings.

Unfortunately the wide curves of the prototype ensure that a very large amount of space would be needed for a true-to-scale model, so the plan shows a slightly modified version. It is possible to sub-divide such a layout so it can be taken to exhibitions but in this instance the scenic arrangements are such that it would be visually unattractive since the model must be built to be viewed from the inside. This is not necessarily a fault, but a more serious consideration is the poor use of the space implicit in the attempt to keep to the wide sweeping curves of the original. Indeed, in this instance I fitted the room around the plan, for if one is attempting to make a model of an irregularly–shaped station, clearly one either needs a very large amount of space, or a purpose-built structure designed to house the model, and one would need to win a major prize on the pools for this!

Plan No. 21 St Piran
OO gauge 3.38 m × 2.175 m; Steam motive power; **Country of origin** Britain (Cornwall);

Other recommended gauges HO, N; **Minimum radius** 600 mm; **Train length** 4 coaches; Medium points; Modification of St Ives plan, with additional scenic features.

Here I have taken the layout of **St Ives** and adapted it to a more geometric pattern and arranged convenient-sized sectional baseboards and altered a lot of the scenic features. The result is **St Piran**, a station with all the advantages of St Ives and none of the snags.

The changes can be considerable. For example, the locomotive depot is not essential, so this section can be omitted to save space. At the same time the inset shows a reverse corner which can be added in place of the present one so that the model can be more conveniently shown at an exhibition, with the operators standing behind the backscene and the visitors looking at the inside of the model. This curve provides an excellent place for modelling a group of small buildings which, if the implied Cornish theme is followed, can be taken from actual prototypes throughout the delectable duchy.

In fact, one advantage of using a prototype layout plan for an imaginary station is that you are no longer tied to the prototype surroundings. There is more scenic detail in the second plan for one simple reason; I could not, quickly, locate much off-stage information on **St Ives** and, since I was not modelling it, I did not bother to go any further. I do know that above **St Ives** there is only a strip of fairly uninteresting Edwardian houses. Behind St Piran there is a bit of the old town, with a medieval gateway which is not only an attractive model, but also takes the road off-stage without any awkward problems on the backscene. I have also included a corner of a castle, which can be intact or ruined according to taste, and a mass of other detail besides. The point is you are free to make alterations to suit your fancy, which you cannot do on a prototype station.

I don't propose to come down on either side. Modelling an actual prototype calls for a good deal of discipline and dedication, but the end product, if properly carried out, must command repect. It is accurate.

Even where you do not follow a prototype

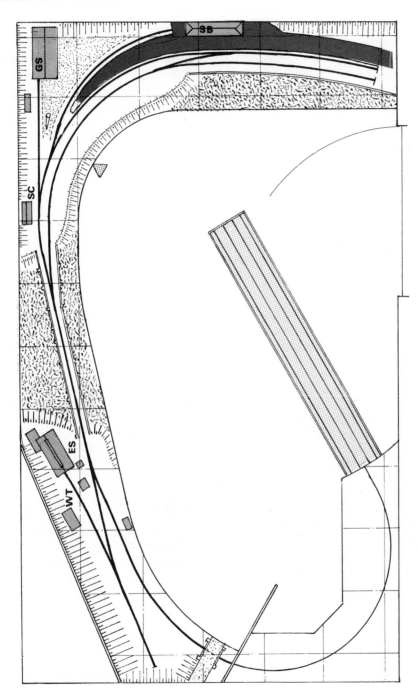

Plan 20   St Ives

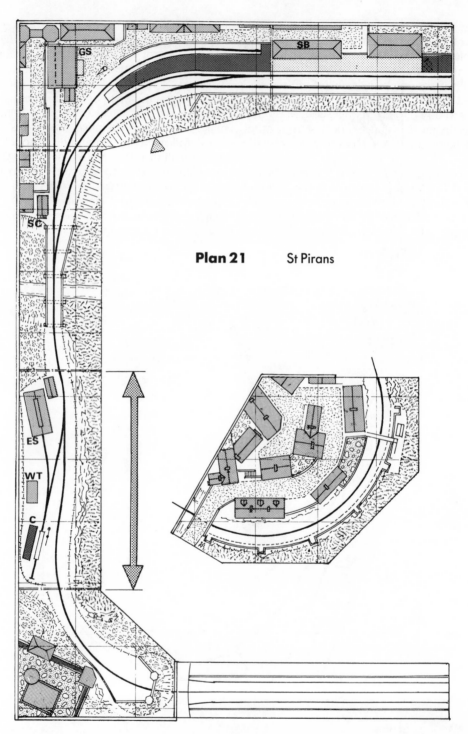

Plan 21   St Pirans

slavishly, it is still a good idea to base the layout, however loosely, on an actual station to give you a sensible starting point. Indeed all the layout plans in this book are based on prototype practice, even if the tracks have been twisted and squeezed to fit the space, and the facilities have been pared down to ease congestion, as is often the case. In most instances, details from other stations have also been incorporated into the plan.

Strict prototype modelling is not too much of a chore if one prefers the present-day scene. I know that most modern trains are very long, but N gauge is well-suited to modern traction requirements. A lot of research appears to be inevitable for the steam age, but as I said at the start, there are illustrated books available to answer a lot of your queries, often before you realize you need to ask the question.

Never let research interfere with modelling. Start work at the first possible moment, as soon as you have the actual track plan. If need be make two models: an initial essay to test techniques, followed by a definitive model incorporating all that has been learned from the first, including the information freely given to you once the first is finished, but which you'd vainly sought beforehand. Remember: Murphy's Law states that essential information on a prototype only comes to light after the model is built.

CHAPTER 5
The potential of N gauge

Probably the best answer to a chronic lack of space is to go to N gauge where one can fit roughly *four times* as much railway into a given space. Although the linear scale of N is approximately half that of OO or HO, layouts occupy an area, and so we square the reduction. This is obvious enough once it has been pointed out, but not quite so apparent beforehand.

The following schemes show how N gauge offers very appreciable advantages in this direction. There are some snags and one is that it does not have the selection of stock available in OO or HO. True enough, but if, in the immediate post war period, we had been offered *half* the choice now available for N we would have thought the Millenium was to hand! Much more to the point, there is more than enough available to provide a good varied selection of stock on a moderately-sized model.

Another objection is cost, since a lot of N gauge equipment is more expensive than its equivalent in OO or HO. However, it is worthwhile considering how much it would cost to acquire a railway room large enough to accommodate the same layout in OO.

Most plans in this book have been drawn for OO or HO gauge. These can be adapted to N by halving the linear measurements, providing one does not reduce operating wells by the same proportions. This brings me directly to an important factor in layout design, the size of the human body.

It is all too easy to overlook the fact that a good model railway fits its owner. Whilst the question of personal choice is difficult to determine, the purely physical limits are well known. I have already pointed out that there is a practical limit to the distance one can effectively reach across a baseboard, and equally there are practical limits on the overall size of a baseboard. As a result, most of the plans so far have been arranged to fit on to a specific size of baseboard, and so it makes sense to see what we can get on these baseboards in the smaller scale.

Plan No. 22   Forge
N gauge 1.20 m × 0.60 m; Steam motive power; **Country of origin** Britain; **Other recommended gauges** Z; **Minimum radius** 175 mm; **Train length** 4 coaches; Large points; Small solid baseboard double track N gauge system.

Plan 22   Forge

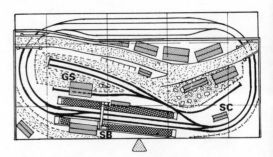

In Plan No. 22, in a space rather less than that occupied by **Lochaber**, we have a double track oval with a reasonable replica of a through station with goods yard, together with storage loops at the rear. There is reasonable scope for scenic modelling, whilst the baseboard is small enough to be easily carried around. As a single unit, **Forge** will not quite fit into a Mini, but if arranged to fold in the centre it can readily be stowed away in the smallest of cars and taken to an exhibition, together with its stock, the control panel and power supplies.

I suggest a separate control panel since in the home one would naturally operate from the front, but at an exhibition you would stand at the back to give the visitors the best view.

Unfortunately, the operational potential of such a line is still somewhat limited and in time one could well tire of the model. There are then two alternatives. Either sell the model as a going concern, or simply build another, in which case wrap the model in transparent polythene sheeting, seal the joints with sticky tape to keep out the dust, and put it in the loft.

Plan No. 23 Beal

N gauge 3.00 m × 0.70 m; Steam motive power; **Country of origin** Britain; **Other recommended gauges** Z; **Minimum radius** 500 mm; **Train length** 5 coaches; Large points; N gauge main line terminus on three baseboards.

Our second N gauge layout is far less likely to go stale. On a pair of metre-long baseboards, which will fit into a small hatchback, one can accommodate a moderately large main line terminus,

whilst a third metre-long section incorporates a fiddle yard. In **Beal** we see a further variation on the fiddle yard theme, the train turntable. This is generally more conveniently arranged in N than in any other gauge, if only because even the modest 0.9 m turntable shown here needs a fair amount of space in which to swing and when one needs 2 m or more, this can be a very considerable problem indeed.

Beal incorporates a centre locomotive release load in the main platforms and an independent run-round loop for the goods yard. Indeed, there are few tricky shunting moves involved and in this respect operation is perhaps a trifle on the easy side. However, the sheer size of the facilities will, I feel, largely offset this.

I have shown very simple station buildings and little in the way of scenic suggestions. When using a uniform scale, drawing intricate detail in what is effectively half the scale of the OO models is not only rather difficult, it is also self-defeating, since when reduced to the standard scale most of the detail is going to end up as a blob.

The next two plans use a very convenient baseboard, a standard flush panelled door. There are a couple of things to note here. The first is that either you need to shorten a second-hand door, or to buy the smallest flush door you can find in the DIY superstore: otherwise you will never get the layout out of the room. The second is that you will find it very difficult to pin anything to the hardboard facing of your door.

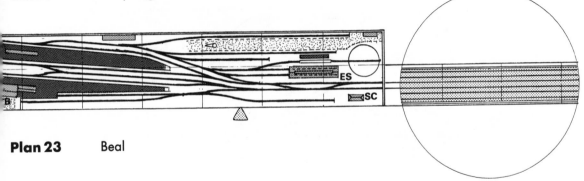

Plan 23   Beal

You should therefore cover one side with insulation board, sticking it down with plenty of PVA woodworking adhesive.

Plan No. 24   Endor

N gauge 2.00 m × 0.75 m; Open motive power; **Country of origin** Britain; **Other recommended gauges** Z; **Minimum radius** 225 mm; **Train length** 7 coaches; Large points; N gauge looped eight with through roads in station built on door.

Endor is a fairly simple, scenic layout designed to allow the 'railway in the landscape' type of model to be constructed on a single baseboard. A four-road through station is provided to allow for a reasonable number of trains, and there is a terminal bay and a reverse loop feature. Even so, capacity is limited, but so long as we are using a solid door as a baseboard we are prevented from having low-level storage sidings. To do this would involve adopting an open-frame construction, preferably of ply, and making provision for access to the lower tracks. Furthermore, such a layout would be a more or less permanent installation, partly on the grounds of weight, but mainly because of another limitation inherent in all readily movable layouts.

It is fairly obvious that you cannot lift up a layout with all the stock on it and expect the models to stay upon the baseboard, let alone on the tracks! The five-train capacity of **Endor** is roughly the amount of stock one can readily replace each operating session.

Plan No. 25   Colstead

N gauge 2.00 m × 0.75 m; Steam motive power; **Country of origin** Britain; **Other recommended gauges** Z; **Minimum radius** 200 mm; **Train length** 7 coaches; Large points; N gauge out-and-back system with continuous run built on door.

The same consideration applies to the second door-sized layout, Plan No. 25, but it is a completely different pattern, a high level terminus with a low-level through station on the continuous run. Once again, a reverse loop is provided to return the trains to the terminus and, once more, the practical limit is four or five trains. The station plan is definitely reminiscent of those produced by Edward Beal, so I have used one of his station names, **Colstead**. However, I didn't crib; I just used the same source as he did for the locomotive shed plan and a lot else beside.

It is very easy to criticize a lot of his later work, where his layout plans for OO took up more room than many of us could ever hope to own, and appeared to need quantities of stock far beyond all practical limits — in the 1950s! Today, when there is a tendency for most of us to have far more stock than we can possibly use, his schemes take on a more practical aspect, particularly where N gauge is concerned.

Plan No. 26   Ennals

N gauge 2.55 m × 2.4 m; Steam motive power; **Country of origin** Britain; **Other recommended**

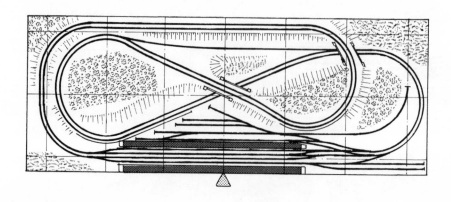

Plan 24
Endor

Plan 25
Colstead

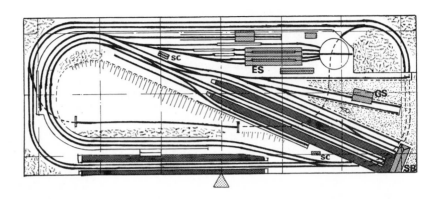

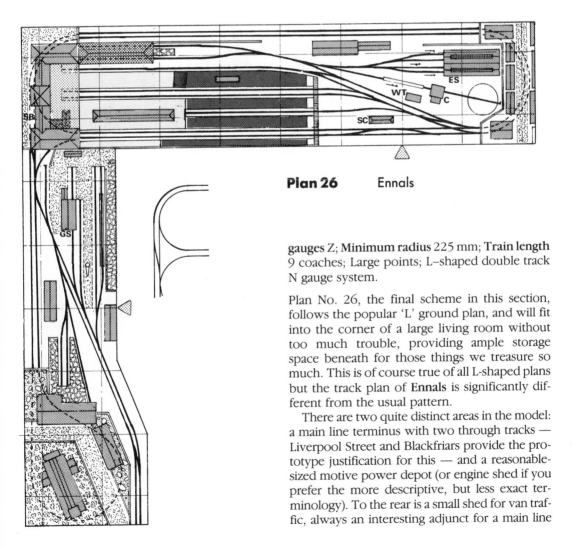

Plan 26   Ennals

gauges Z; **Minimum radius** 225 mm; **Train length** 9 coaches; Large points; L–shaped double track N gauge system.

Plan No. 26, the final scheme in this section, follows the popular 'L' ground plan, and will fit into the corner of a large living room without too much trouble, providing ample storage space beneath for those things we treasure so much. This is of course true of all L-shaped plans but the track plan of **Ennals** is significantly different from the usual pattern.

There are two quite distinct areas in the model: a main line terminus with two through tracks — Liverpool Street and Blackfriars provide the prototype justification for this — and a reasonable-sized motive power depot (or engine shed if you prefer the more descriptive, but less exact terminology). To the rear is a small shed for van traffic, always an interesting adjunct for a main line station. At right angles there is a moderately-sized goods yard with coal drops, a conventional goods shed and a set of loading docks associated with a large warehouse. These two distinct elements are linked by hidden loops.

As most N gauge stock will take a fairly sharp corner, it makes it practicable, on a 600 mm wide baseboard, to make a complete U–turn, but the visual effect is hardly realistic. However, only a small proportion of the layout is set out in this way and it is fairly simple to hide these sections under high-level townscapes. Where a complete reverse loop is involved, there is room for a very small church standing in a slightly cramped churchyard to go above the tracks. This is one of the side advantages of N, one can make a true-to-scale model of a parish church that does not so dominate the layout that everyone assumes it's a cathedral.

Z gauge offers slightly more scope in a given space than N, but is rather limited in application by the fact that only one major manufacturer, Marklin, has developed the size. So one is primarily restricted to a German prototype, which does tend to narrow the scope. If this is your choice then you simply use N scale plans, as the extra room thus obtained is always welcome. Z is fairly costly, but the quality is superb, and you cannot expect to get Mercedes-Benz quality at Volkswagen prices!

Visually, 2 mm scale is little different from N, but the use of finer wheels and closer tolerances does make it inadvisable to adopt the tight curves shown in these plans. I have it on good authority that a 450 mm radius is as tight as one should go and so 2 mm is not quite so suited for a very compact layout as N, which can take fairly sharp corners with ease.

CHAPTER 6

On narrow tracks

A solution to the perennial problem of getting a lot of layout into a small space is to adopt narrow gauge. Unfortunately, a few years ago this was badly overdone, and a plethora of very indifferent models appeared on the exhibition circuit. Indeed, to one slightly cynical observer, a lot of modellers — if that is the correct term — decided that as a lot of narrow gauge lines were semi-derelict, one could make rough and ready models and get away with it. This is a fallacy, since rough and ready narrow gauge looks bad and runs badly. If this is the way you think, stick to toy trains instead.

I am not criticizing the use of narrow gauge to produce a layout with a high fun content, providing the modelling is also of high quality. Indeed, there is a strong element of amusement in the first three schemes in this chapter whilst they exploit models which are reasonably easy to obtain from specialized suppliers, or more conveniently, at the major exhibitions with a good trade support. Nevertheless, we should never lose sight of the fact that with so varied a prototype, which in most cases has very limited amounts of rolling stock, narrow gauge can be a haven for the keen scratchbuilder or kit basher.

Plan No. 27   Bad Schmelling
HOe gauge 1.20 m × 0.725 m; Open motive power; **Country of origin** Austria; **Other recommended gauges** 009; **Minimum radius** 175 mm;

Train length 4 coaches; Small points; Compact narrow gauge looped eight 'rabbit' layout.

With all this in mind, Plan No. 27 is supposed to be somewhere in Austria, where 750 mm gauge is still very much in evidence. I am suggesting this locale for **Bad Schmelling** because not only are some rather nice Austrian narrow gauge models available, but it is a little easier to accept the mountainous scenery implicit in this simplified 'rabbit' layout. A rabbit layout, I should explain, is one which has lots of tunnels into which trains pop in and out with complete abandon. The scheme is intended to use HO stock on 9 mm gauge, HOe to be precise, but as with other narrow gauge designs, any of the recognized narrow gauge arrangements can be used.

Plan 27   Bad Schmelling

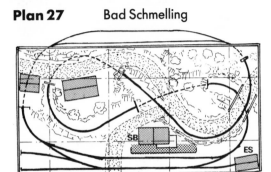

Plan No. 28 Kleine Freidegg
HOm gauge 1.35 m × 1.05 m; Electric motive power; **Country of origin** Switzerland; **Other recommended gauges** OOn3, HOn3; **Minimum radius** 350 mm; **Train length** 3 coaches; Medium points; Metre gauge looped eight plan in minimum space.

This follows Swiss metre gauge practice — at a respectable distance! Here again, a good selection of suitable models is available from Bemo through a few specialist firms in Britain. The particular plan was originally worked out for OO or HO, and appears as such in my earlier planbook, *60 Plans for Small Railways* (published by Peco), but it is rather toylike in that gauge. Swiss metre gauge is much more realistic, the prototype does behave rather like this. **Kleine Freidegg** also provides a suitable test bed for an Alpine scheme to determine the best scenic techniques to follow before you move on to a more ambitious prototypical layout, on the lines of some schemes later in this book.

These two schemes are compact, readily moved about and fairly typical narrow gauge 'fun' layouts, not really intended to be taken as strict prototypical models. Narrow gauge can be a more serious business, so we now turn to an attempt to reproduce the spirit of an actual narrow gauge railway in a moderate-sized site. We also allow ourselves a little historical fiction because, even when following prototype practice, model railways should be fun.

Plan No. 29 Porthaddog
009 gauge 2.25 m × 1.80 m; Steam motive power; **Country of origin** Wales; **Other recommended gauges** HOe; **Minimum radius** 180 mm; **Train length** 4 coaches; Medium points; Elaborate narrow gauge system inspired by Festiniog — at a distance.

So for Plan No. 29 we assume that early in the nineteenth century, a Mr Haddock realized the commercial potential of the slate that makes up so many Welsh mountains, and not only built a 2 ft gauge railway up into the mountains, but also constructed a port on the coast. The name has been slightly changed with the upsurge of Welsh consciousness, and is now **Porthaddog**.

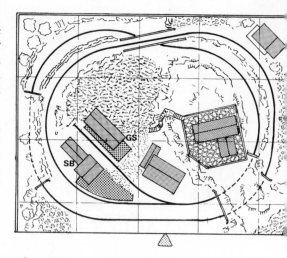

Plan 28   Kleine Freidegg

There is only a loose parallel with the Festiniog, which certainly does not have a large viaduct, nor does it snake down the hillside with successive loops. The terminus owes more to Scotland and the Cambletown and Machrihanish than Wales, but having said all that, the layout does allow for a fairly intensive traffic up and down the hill. To deal with the difference in levels, there are a couple of hidden tracks which additionally incorporate passing loops for train storage. These are placed behind the backscene and will be invisible to the operator, with every opportunity for dire goings on.

There are two ways around this problem. A few strategically placed car wing mirrors plus some effective lighting will give the operators a view of the models. This is the simplest arrangement, but will almost certainly be tiring since a good deal of squinting will be required. A more satisfactory arrangement involves some form of track circuits, which could be arranged by setting light-dependent resistors in the tracks, coupled with a suitable solid state amplifier either to work LED indicators on the panel, or a separate large light panel, possibly incorporating 12 v lamps worked through relays. It would even be possible to automate this part of the layout, providing you were so minded or had a

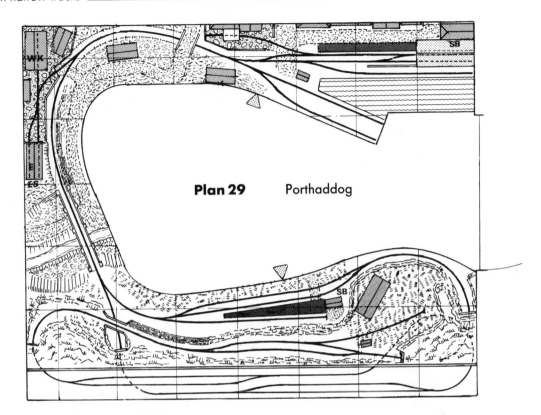

Plan 29   Porthaddog

tame boffin on hand prepared to do the work. The only snag here is that this particular breed of railway modeller has one potential flaw, a tendency to use a mainframe computer to do the work of an on-off switch. This would be acceptable, if it always worked, but Murphys Law has it that not only will something go wrong, but also that it will happen just when your boffin has taken up an exciting new post in Saudi Arabia or somewhere equally inaccessible.

However, back to narrow gauge as a prototype for a serious model railway. Or is serious the word I really want? You see, full-size narrow gauge can and frequently does do things that one might feel are rather too toy-like to be believed. Nowhere is this more apparent than in Switzerland. In my travels over the Swiss metre gauge I have constantly been struck by the fact that the stations appear to have been designed by a modeller with few inhibitions. So, when I

decided to conclude with a prototype which looked more like a model railway, I was spoilt for choice. Finally, I decided to use **Gais**, on the St Gallen – Gais – Appenzell Bahn.

Plan No. 30a Gais (1)
HOm gauge 3.70 m × 1.90 m; Electric motive power; **Country of origin** Switzerland; **Other recommended gauges** OOn3; HOn3; **Minimum radius** 300 mm; **Train length** 3 coaches; Medium points; Close copy of station on metre gauge SGA, Appenzell.

This pair of plans is included to demonstrate some of the problems of following an actual prototype. On the ground, it looks almost as if **Gais** will fit comfortably on to a small solid baseboard, but as Plan No. 30a shows, it will not. Yes, the track does turn a half circle and the turnout into the depot is at the end of the curve, and handworked into the bargain. The branch to

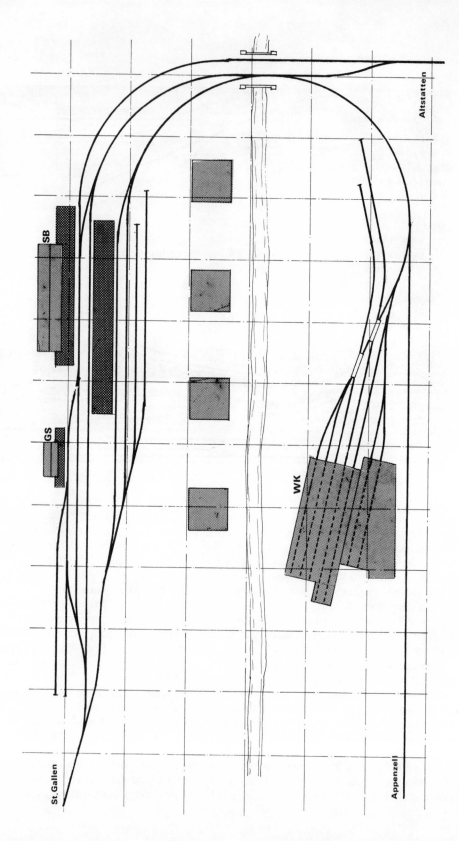

Plan 30a
Gais (1)

Aldstatten does head off like that and the stream and house are there as shown. Truly, there is prototype for everything! The plan, incidentally, is based on a diagram in *Appenzellerland mit Bahn und Bus* by Gustav F. Rohr (available in specialist railway bookshops), and is only approximately to scale. Even so, it is a trifle too big for comfort.

Plan No. 30b Gais (2)
HOm gauge 3.00 m × 2.10 m; Electric motive power; **Country of origin** Switzerland; **Other recommended gauges** HOn3; **Minimum radius** 480 mm; **Train length** 3 coaches; Medium points; Reduced plan of Gais station with offstage loops.

So in Plan No. 30b I show a slightly compressed version of the original. The loops are still capable of handling the three-coach trains of the prototype and the station layout is according to the sketch plan I am working from. The depot is simplified. I had little qualm since my recollections of the depot do not agree with the plan in the book, though to be fair I visited the place half-way through reconstruction.

This plan also shows a series of offstage loops which not only allows the line to be worked as the prototype, but also permits a good deal of fun running as well. I do not see why one should not 'play trains' now and then, providing the model can be operated in accordance with prototype practice. After all, the Appenzeller

Plan 30b   Gais (2)

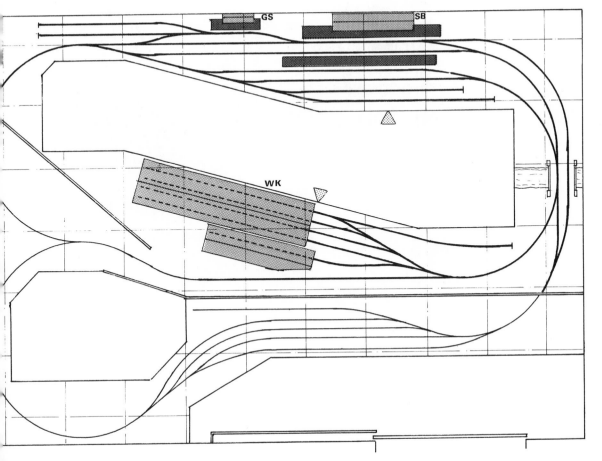

Bahnen do run a very businesslike railway and work the system in a professional fashion. They also like to hang on to vintage stock, and positively overwhelm any visiting party with hospitality.

Once again, the room had to be fitted around the plan, but it is not an uncommon size. I've suggested a sliding door, a practicable alternative to the usual swinging version which tends to make things a trifle difficult at times.

Before we leave narrow gauge, there are a couple of things worth pointing out. Narrow gauge station layouts do not differ materially from standard gauge single track practice of the country concerned. The main differences, apart from length of loops and the radius involved, concern the signalling which will almost certainly be simplified and may even be absent altogether. So a lot of the single track OO layouts in this book are adaptable to narrow gauge. Second, although there are several distinct varieties of narrow gauge, all these plans are equally suited to any scale/gauge combination you happen to favour, though those for O (32 mm) and 1 (45 mm) gauges are more applicable to the garden than indoor locations.

CHAPTER 7
The second smallest room

In most British homes there is a small room over the entrance hall which is loosely described as the third bedroom. Only the fact that house specifications are not covered by the Trades Description Act allows estate agents and builders to get away with this, though estate agent Roy Brooks, who made a point of injecting candour into his advertisements, did once suggest that it would best suit a small child or dwarf. To this he could well have added 'or model railway' for my observations suggest that, if any room is free inside the house for our hobby, then this is it. At first sight its small size appears to restrict one's choice but, as I shall be showing, it offers a wide range of alternatives. I am using, throughout this chapter, the same room plan, based on just such a room in a former home of mine. The second restriction is the doorway.

Most room doors open inward: obvious, but for our purposes very awkward. Some modellers have re-hung the door to open outward, but I would not advise this since there is a very good reason for the convention. In most homes the upper landing is down to the barest minimum size already and you do not want any more obstructions. The best arrangement, a sliding door, is ruled out in this instance since there is generally a low bulkhead in the corner of the room to accommodate the stair head. So I have instead chosen the easy option and designed the layouts to allow the door to open normally and, where possible, allow for entry whilst the

layout is in operation.

If this is impracticable, a lift-out section is needed. I do not advise a hinged flap since this is a more difficult device to arrange particularly if you intend to put scenic features on it. A relatively short section less than a metre long which can be built on light framing and be supported on two short battens, provided with location dowels, is easily lifted off and slid on to prepared runners underneath one section of baseboard for storage.

Plan No. 31   Buchan (for Tweedsmuir)
OO gauge 2.40 m × 1.95 m; Diesel motive power; **Country of origin** Scotland; **Other recommended gauges** HO, N*; **Minimum radius** 600 mm; **Train length** 3 coaches; Medium points; Scotsrail terminus, based loosely on Thurso, ca 1986.

This plan is a diesel era layout on which scale-length, locomotive-hauled trains can be run. **Buchan (for Tweedsmuir)** exploits the fact that Scotsrail, until the advent of modern DMUs, ran the Highland section mainly with trains consisting of three Mk1 BR coaches headed by a class 37. As Lima currently offer these in Scotsrail livery, it would be little short of churlish not to produce a scheme to take advantage of this largess. Then there is the fact that the Highlands make a superb setting for a model railway.

There is a small terminus close to a loch, any

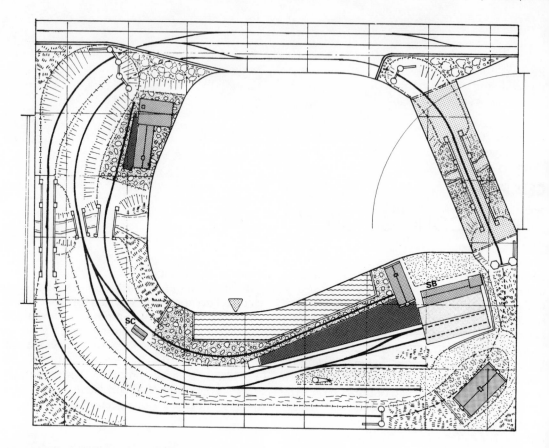

Plan 31   Buchan (for Tweedsmuir)

similarity between this and the layout at Thurso being quite intentional. There is a siding feeding a distillery, to take advantage not only of the fact that branded grain hoppers are used on this traffic and are, once again, available in model form, but also that research into the prototype industry is doubly rewarding as a visit to the premises usually ends with a wee dram! And, of course, it is pleasing to have the prototype there in the form you want it. Quite like old times.

Accepted practice today would take the line round to a simple fiddle yard and stop there. I prefer to include a continuous run to allow one to see the trains moving around the Scottish landscape, passing en route over a pair of fine bridges. The Highland lines have plenty of superb prototypes to choose from, and once

again, it would be folly not to take advantage of this. The harbour, I am told, is not too confined for one of Mr McBrayne's smaller ferries, though when designing it I had trawlers in mind. Fish is a useful traffic for a railway.

If you want to be strictly correct, the overall roof ought to be more or less out of use with the tracks stopping short, but space in this small room is at a premium. You must spruce up the old station building, for this is an important characteristic of Scotsrail, many structures having now had their first proper attention in half a century. You will notice a tower in one corner. Highland termini generally possessed a clock tower, but nowadays the clock is not guaranteed to be in working order. How like the model!

Should you prefer a steam-age model, a few

changes must be made. For a start, the Highland preferred tender locomotives, usually distinctive 4-4-0s with resounding Highland names. The distillery will have to go to make room for the turntable and you may wish to re-arrange the fiddle sidings to accommodate a second table.

Plan No. 32 Aylbury

OO gauge 2.40 m × 1.95 m; Open motive power; **Country of origin** Britain; **Other recommended gauges** HO, N*; **Minimum radius** 600 mm; **Train length** 3 coaches; Medium points; Development of Deane pattern fiddle yard in small bedroom.

Plan No. 32 began as a variant on the Deane type fiddle yard with the loops behind the station, but, as happens from time to time with my plans,

Aylbury insisted on developing and I was not prepared to stop it. So the single track branch now runs into a larger junction station which does make more sense operationally.

The main attention is however focused on the branch terminus, a reasonably commodious one with an interesting array of facilities. In particular, the goods shed is on the other side of the station to the yard proper which adds a pleasing difference to the pattern of shunting. There is a low backscene to hide the fiddle tracks, but in later schemes with this arrangement, I suggest other ways of hiding these roads.

The through station is extremely simple, with a small goods facility, comprising one shed and a short coal drop. There is a storage siding, which is capable of taking a short branch train of, say, two coaches. The station building is of the over-

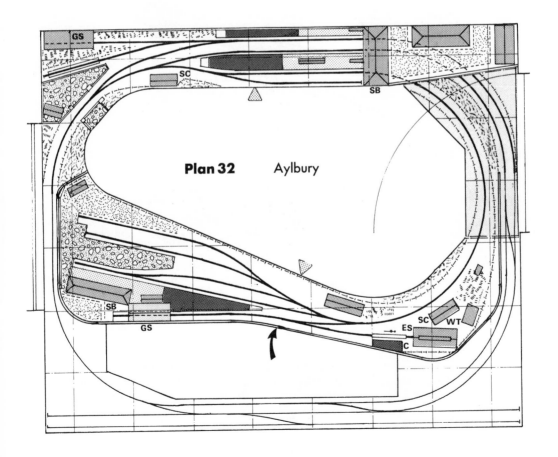

Plan 32   Aylbury

track pattern more commonly associated with urban sites, and so I have utilized the corner to provide a station square of sorts, complete with large shops, offices, public buildings or what-you-will.

An interesting feature of this layout is that it could, if you wished, be operated from behind the terminus, since the majority of train movements at the junction can just as readily be controlled from a distance. This would make it very effective for viewers, who under the over-riding control of the main operator could be allowed to do a little shunting at the junction.

Plan No. 33 Brookside

OO gauge 2.40 m × 1.95 m; Open motive power; Country of origin Britain; Other recommended gauges HO, N*; Minimum radius 600 mm; Train length 3 coaches; Medium points; Suburban system operated with tank engines.

I firmly believe that unless there is easy access to all tracks, performance will suffer. The design of Aylbury has this in mind, and in Plan No. 33 we look at this important design requirement in a different fashion.

Brookside has one of my favourite arrangements, an out-and-back scheme incorporating a continuous run on two levels, so that there is a sort of triangular junction between the terminus and the main line loop. This is both visually attractive and operationally convenient. The underlying idea is a small terminus which is served by two single track routes. There are just the two main platform roads, but the other road is the goods shunting neck. A loop is provided

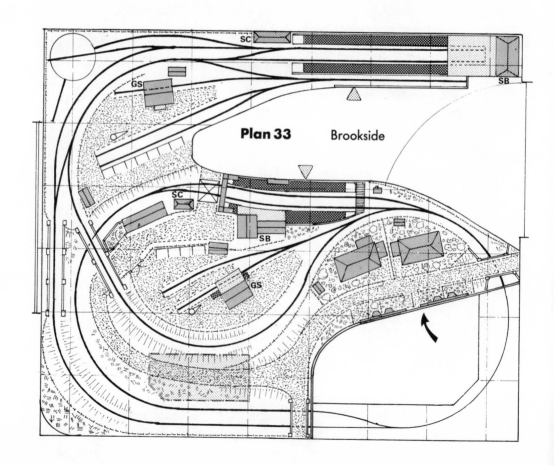

Plan 33   Brookside

around the curve rather than in the platform roads. This, in my opinion, is a far better arrangement, as the platforms can double as carriage storage tracks without impairing operation. Simple locomotive valeting facilities are provided, while the turntable is only large enough for a 4-4-0 or 2-6-0.

There are two turnouts just at the extreme limit of easy access and so I would make part of the main terminus goods yard on a removable baseboard to give proper access to this part of the model. Of course, if the tracks are properly installed in the first instance, there should be very little trouble here but, as I have already mentioned, Murphy's Law rules all model railways, and can only be effectively circumvented by ensuring that trouble is easily dealt with before it becomes chronic.

The second feature is a conventional single track passing station with a small goods yard. There is a typical piece of suburban development nearby, with fully–modelled bungalows and low-relief semi-detached houses. This occupies one corner, though it is a long walk to the nearby station. No doubt the estate agent described these highly desirable properties as being within a stone's throw of the station and took good care to take any prospective buyers to the site in his car!

The large open well at the rear gives access to the further turnout on the main line, whilst a lift-out section of scenery allows one to reach the furthest tracks for regular cleaning.

Plan No. 34 Trent
OO gauge 2.40 m × 1.95 m; Open motive

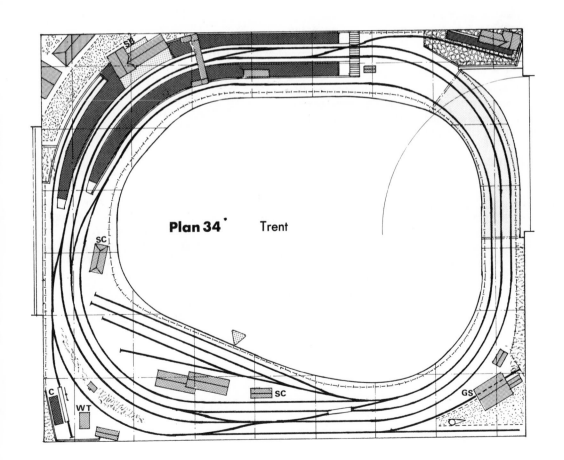

Plan 34 Trent

power; **Country of origin** Britain; **Other recommended gauges** HO, EM, N*; **Minimum radius** 600 mm; **Train length** 6 coaches; Medium points; Three track scheme capable of handling long trains.

Trent is strictly a main line which will take up to five coach trains if desired. The secret is a highly unconventional fiddle yard in the form of an inner reversible track provided with a fan of sidings which can be used to store stock.

Trent has a miniscule goods yard, more for cosmetic effect and the provision of a little shunting than anything else. Further intricate shunting is provided by the private siding near the doorway. Here we have the unusual, but absolutely correct arrangement of a trailing point leading to a crossing that runs straight into the siding, which would only be shunted outside the busy hours. The trailing crossover in the platform roads is strictly optional. It is worth pointing out that a facing lead into the private siding from the outer rail is barred, not so much by the old Board of Trade regulations, but by the fact that such sidings can only be effectively worked when arranged to trail. Otherwise, the locomotive is in the way when you want to drop a wagon or van into the factory. As the platform has to be on a curve, I have increased the radius to reduce the inevitable gap between coaches and the platform edge.

Plan No. 35   Umberleigh
OO gauge 2.40 m × 1.95 m; Steam motive power; **Country of origin** Britain (Wessex); **Other recommended gauges** HO, EM, N*; **Minimum radius** 600 mm; **Train length** 4 coaches; Medium points; Looped eight, single track system with ample landscape features.

In Plan No. 35, **Umberleigh**, we have an old friend, the looped eight. There are storage roads under the main station, these are shown below the main plan for the sake of clarity. For obvious reasons, it would be as well to build the station above on a couple of lightweight sub-baseboards that can be removed for maintenance. In any case, you would use an open framing, with the loops on narrow bases to allow access from underneath for cleaning, fishing out derailed

stock and the like. As before, the platform is on a larger radius curve.

This is essentially a layout on which to watch trains go by, and would be greatly improved by as elaborate a measure of remote control as you care to devise. It would be a good candidate for computer control, particularly as the monitor could then give details of the next train. This would greatly impress visitors until something went wrong, and the announcement of a through train from London was followed by the appearance of the local pick-up freight. The trouble with computers is that they assume things go as they say, whereas model railways often appear to have a mind of their own!

The yard is large enough to give the air of accuracy, though in full size the sidings would be at least twice as long. The outer siding is just a storage road, extremely useful and, with a train of coaches upon it, very decorative into the bargain.

The crossover in the centre of the loop was standard prototype practice, and it allowed a locomotive to run round a train without the need to have possession of both stretches of main line. It is arranged so that passenger trains may pass whilst part of the loop is blocked by shunting movements. On the prototype this would rarely be the case, but on model railways we like to maintain the sort of service more commonly associated with the London Underground in the rush hour.

Access to the goods yard is by means of a level crossing which, unusually, is not supervised closely by a signal box. As it is solely for access to the yard, and is not on an adopted road, no gates are needed, though there is no doubt that they do look pretty. However, as we have three level crossings on public roads which must be gated, there is no point in being greedy.

At the point where the rising and falling tracks are on roughly the same level, I show a road with two level crossings in succession, sharing the single crossing keeper's cottage since two cottages, so close together, would look a trifle odd. The crossing keeper will certainly have a very busy, not to say strenuous life, but further round the corner there is a single set of gates where the keeper can enjoy life and have more time to tend

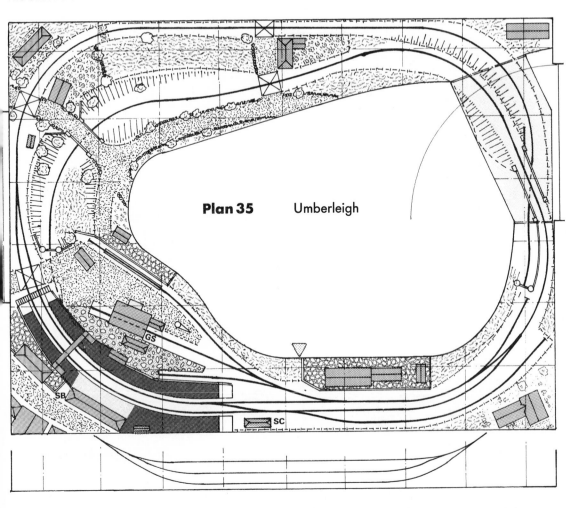

Plan 35   Umberleigh

his garden. The object of all this has been to provide a section of railway in landscape. This is a very valid part of our hobby, providing it is not carried out to the point where one needs to search assiduously for the railway amongst the scenic extravaganza.

All the tracks are within easy reach of the operating space, though the townscape beyond the station is a trifle out of reach. I would advise constructing it on a piece of plywood cut to fit and capable of being dropped in place without too much difficulty. With this in mind, it would be best to arrange the ply base and its locating nubs before tracklaying began rather than leaving it until you get down to scenic construction.

Plan No. 36   Enborough
N/2 mm gauge 2.40 m × 1.95 m; Diesel motive power; **Country of origin** Britain; **Other recommended gauges** Z; **Minimum radius** 180 mm; **Train length** 8 coaches; Large points; N gauge main line system in small bedroom with extensive looping.

The final scheme for the small bedroom, Plan No. 36 switches to N gauge, partly to demonstrate the enormous difference where even a modest space is concerned. Here we do have a fully–fledged modern layout, for **Enborough** can comfortably take nine coach trains behind a large diesel. Low-level loops provide

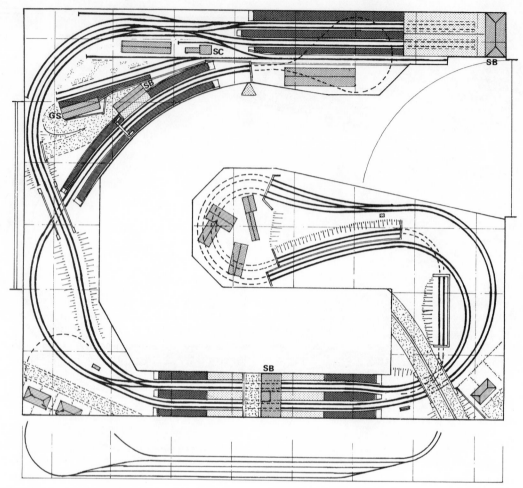

Plan 36   Enborough

ample train storage, and the four track terminus is also capacious. Most of all, the track convolutions do allow for some fairly varied running around the extensive main line. Visible curves range from the easy to very easy, the only tight ones being decently hidden under a model farmyard. I have only sketched in the main buildings, although there is ample room here for a fully-fledged model of a small farm complex.

The tracks are crossed by a section of modern dual carriageway road. I would cone off one lane, and then stage a crash, with the complimentary shunt on the opposing section caus-

ed by a couple of rubber–necking drivers looking at the accident. This would neatly account for the fact that nothing is actually moving.

Even with the extra scope of N, space is still a trifle limited, and this, not to mention all other layouts in this chapter, would be improved if a slightly larger area was available. I have set the size at that of the smallest small bedroom I have ever owned, but conversation in the Model Railway Club suggests that I may have been slightly over-generous. All I can say is that in my considered opinion, any room smaller than this is only an overgrown cupboard.

CHAPTER 8
The business of portability

My trusty *Concise Oxford Dictionary* defines portable as *Movable (article), convenient for carrying.* The last three words are vital, since without them we could define a rubbish skip as portable! However, what is or is not convenient is something else. Many years ago, Peter Denny suggested that a portable baseboard should not exceed 4 × 2 ft (1.2 × 0.6 m), as anything larger was usually too heavy and decidedly unwieldy. My own opinion is that nowadays we should define a portable layout as one that fits into the family car. This means that a baseboard measuring 3 × 1 ft 6 in (1 × 0.5 m) is probably more convenient, particularly if we take into account the capacity of current small hatchbacks. Another important consideration is the need to be able to erect the layout, set out the stock, enjoy an interesting operating session, put everything away and still get to bed by midnight at the latest.

Experience shows that it is best to arrange baseboards as mirror image pairs, so that they

can be stored face to face, with a pair of spacers, resulting in an open crate with the delicate models facing inward. If the spacers are bolted to the ends, they also protect the delicate rail ends. Alternatively pairs of baseboards may be hinged together so they may be quickly folded up. In such cases, the maximum length of the section is governed by the need to be able to swing the section up and over, and once again 3 ft (1 m) is probably the practical limit.

Plan No. 37 St Denys
OO gauge 3.00 m × 0.425 m; Steam motive power; **Country of origin** Britain (Cornwall); **Other recommended gauges** O, EM/P4, HO, N; **Minimum radius** 1,000 mm; **Train length** 2 coaches; Large points; Folding layout based on Peter Denny's *Stony Stratford.*

This folding can be carried still further, providing the sections are relatively small, and with Plan No. 37 we have a four-fold scheme. Pro-

Plan 37   St Denys

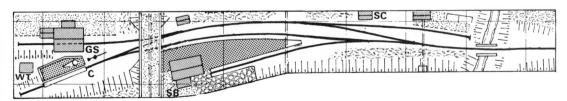

viding the baseboard framing is light, the resulting crate is small enough and light enough to be easily carried around and certainly compact enough to fit into a small hatchback with both seats up.

St Denys is based closely on Peter Denny's Stony Stratford, with the addition of a bay road to increase operating interest. The original was a secondary unit in the first Buckingham layout where its relative simplicity was no disadvantage.

The road bridge lifts off to reveal the main hinges, some 20 to 30 mm above track level, thus providing ample space for the various buildings to fit in between each other. The small hut housing the coal office lifts off to reveal one hinge, the other has to be disguised as best as one can under scenery, where the height above rail is

less. The other hut fits neatly into the valley containing the stream.

This would make an excellent scheme for the younger enthusiast, living at home, in digs or in a university hall of residence, as the main layout is compact enough to fit inside a medium-sized cupboard. It is a trifle restricted in scope, but it is really a case of something being better than nothing. It would also make an excellent first essay in EM or P4, demanding enough to test everything, but not too much to create problems.

Plan No. 38   Yiewsford
OO gauge 2.50 m × 2.00 m; Steam motive power; **Country of origin** Britain; **Other recommended gauges** EM, HO, N; **Minimum radius** 600 mm; **Train length** 4 coaches; Medium

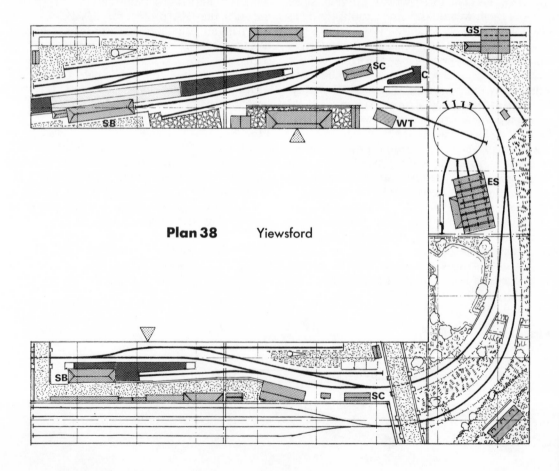

Plan 38   Yiewsford

points; U-shaped portable branch, maximum recommended size.

Plan No. 38 shows what I consider to be the optimum portable design, an U-shaped system built on six 1 × 0.5 m boards. The main station, **Yiewsford**, is a fairly conventional single track terminus with its goods facilities nicely spread about to make life interesting. There is a fairly large locomotive depot which should be cut down if you require complete authenticity, but is still too small to hold all the locomotives one tends to collect for a layout nowadays. You do not have to be too pernickity when following the prototype.

As the line curves round past the locomotive depot, the tracks diverge. The outer goes under a road and straight into a conventional fiddle yard. In front of the fiddle yard is a small 'passing' station with reasonable freight facilities. In practice it is a terminus but as the locomotive spur ends under yet another overbridge the line appears to extend further. This is a particularly useful dodge if you want to avoid having too many termini. It also allows you to consider a further extension to a proper small terminus, possibly for exhibition use only since **Yiewsford** is large enough as it is when erected in a normal living-room or bedroom.

I have sketched in a little scenic development around the main line, proposing a large pond or small lake. A small row of farmworkers' cottages is stuck in the corner. Between the small station and the intermediate backscene a row of houses or shops lines the rather narrow road. These structures could, if you wished, form the backscene at this point. I would suggest that the branch should be on a gentle gradient, raising the small station perhaps 15 mm above the level of the main line and fiddle yard, but this is really a matter of taste.

Plan No. 39 Yeoman's Acre

EM/P4 gauge 3.30 m × 0.45 m; Diesel motive power; **Country of origin** Britain (Somerset); **Other recommended gauges** OO, HO, N; **Minimum radius** 1,000 mm; **Train length** 2 coaches; Scratchbuilt points; Mineral branch with vestigial passenger service.

In 4 mm scale, Plan No. 39 would not be easy to fold around the central bridge and so would best be treated as two separate sections. N gauge would be quite different, of course. Whilst applicable to the steam age, I had a modern situation in mind, where a branch is kept alive solely because of heavy mineral traffic, hence the name, **Yeoman's Acre**. As the branch exists a token DMU service is provided, but the main interest is in the mineral traffic off the loading plant.

As a further flight of fancy, the tracks could be shared by a preservation group, who operate steam trains on Saturdays, Sundays, high days and holidays, and during the week maintain a service with a refurbished DMU in their own livery. This would provide an excuse for owning a wide variety of steam locomotives, since on a preserved line, it is not incongruous to have a large express locomotive travelling tender first at the head of a three-coach train!

One very definite anachronism is the narrow gauge feeder on the high level, as a modern mineral plant would bring the product in on a conveyor belt. In addition, the overtrack loading gantry would incorporate a pair of discontinuous automatic weighing machines and be somewhat larger as a result. In addition, there ought to be a railway weighbridge as a final check on loading, but alas, there isn't room.

Yeoman's Acre introduces the 'kickback' pattern fiddle yard. Unlike a siding, this is a very convenient way of getting a decent fan of sidings within the overall length of a small straight baseboard.

Needless to say, this layout would be ideally suited for exhibition use, where the operator would move round to the rear, not only providing the paying public with a better view but also getting himself better access to the fiddle sidings. In this case, you either need to own a large estate car, or to build it on four baseboards, rearranging the structures to suit. I do not recommend putting a layout on a roof rack; not only is it more vulnerable but, although the weight is well within the carrying limit of the car, the bulk will mean that the aerodynamics will be completely upset, with very adverse results on both fuel consumption and maximum safe speeds. The model will also be exceptionally vulnerable, even when thoroughly wrapped in heavy gauge plastic.

So far we have largely considered the limitations of the portable scheme, we now turn to some positive advantages. First and foremost, portable layouts do not have to be fixed in design, bits can be added or taken away. The obvious solution is to arrange a standardized joint face so that sections can be butted together in any order. This idea has been extensively developed in the USA in the modular system. There is just one thing wrong with this approach — it is unutterably toy-like! Certainly it works, and if you want a glorified train set go ahead; but it is a complete negation of all the best principles of layout design. The prototype does not conform to the fixed geometric arrangements implicit in this system. It was tried in Britain, and quietly forgotten long before the USA even considered the idea.

However, a more cogent argument against this arrangement is that there is a simpler method of connecting a range of stations together that calls for no great pre-planning, places no restrictions whatsoever on design and into the bargain takes care of the rather tricky business of aligning the landscape physically whilst allowing a proper matching of scenic colours. It is the short match section. These are very simple to construct, and I have seen it done in a little under an hour during the setting up of an exhibition, though most of the arrangements I suggest are slightly more complicated than the very straightforward fill-in so produced.

The idea is explored in the sequence of layouts in Plan No. 40, where I have taken four single track stations and linked them with simple pieces of baseboard containing nothing more than plain track and appropriate scenery.

Plan No. 40a Poldark
OO gauge 3.90 m × 1.00 m; Steam motive power; **Country of origin** Britain (Cornwall); **Other recommended gauges** EM, HO, N; **Minimum radius** 600 mm; **Train length** 4 coaches; Medium points; Branch terminus with harbour extension.

We start with Plan No. 40a, a reasonably

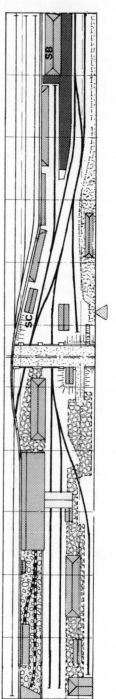

Plan 39
Yeoman's Acre

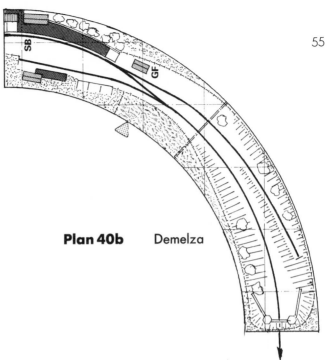

Plan 40b Demelza

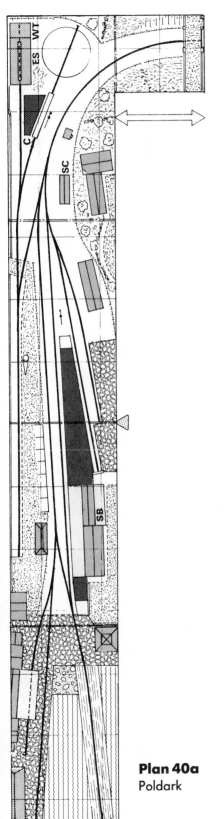

Plan 40a
Poldark

elaborate terminus built on four 1 × 0.5 m baseboards. The only unconventional feature of **Poldark** is the development of the roads beyond the platform end around a small Cornish harbour, complete with a fairly substantial timber jetty. There is, I suggest, a sloping hard at the end of the inlet where small boats can be winched up out of the water, a characteristic feature of most small fishing ports. The coal and cattle sidings are separate and a small locomotive depot completes the picture. The line then curves around a short filler, marked with an open arrow, and disappears under an overbridge, either into the fiddle yard, or the next station.

Plan No. 40b Demelza

OO gauge 1.58 m × 1.58 m; Steam motive power; **Country of origin** Britain (Cornwall); **Other recommended gauges** EM, HO, N; **Minimum radius** 600 mm; **Train length** 4 coaches; Large points; Small halt on curved section with storage siding.

Demelza is a simple halt set on a large radius curve, with a short siding complete with coal bins and a goods platform. The curved baseboards are very effective as a means of breaking up the essentially rectangular arrangement of the usual portable system, this theme

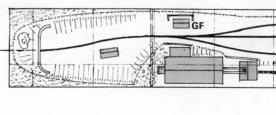

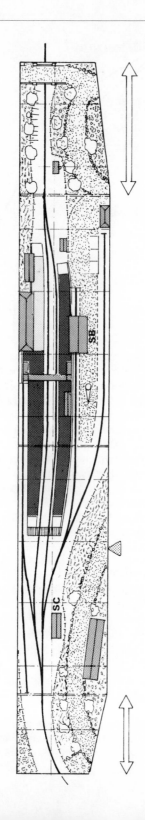

could be developed if desired. One long siding, which can be used to hold spare coaches, runs off level whilst the line drops to go into a tunnel, beyond which you would enter the fiddle yard — or would you?

Plan No. 40c Warleggan
OO gauge 6.90 m × 0.75 m; Steam motive power; **Country of origin** Britain (Cornwall); **Other recommended gauges** EM, HO, N; **Minimum radius** 600 mm; **Train length** 4 coaches; Medium points; Single track passing station.

We could, instead, leave **Poldark** for **Warleggan**, Plan No. 40c, a perfectly conventional single track passing station, of which only the two fill-in sections are worthy of note. On the left the track aligns with **Poldark**, on the right it exits under an overbridge leading either to **Demelza** or the fiddle yard.

Plan No. 40d Wheal Leisure
OO gauge 4.20 m × 1.20 m; Steam motive power; **Country of origin** Britain (Cornwall); **Other recommended gauges** EM, HO, N; **Minimum radius** 600 mm; **Train length** 4 coaches; Medium points; Copper mine with small halt for miners.

Plan No. 40d shows two further sections, a small two-baseboard scheme incorporating a copper mine, **Wheal Leisure**, together with a halt for the miners' trains and a corner section, again on two baseboards depicting the line passing over the head of a creek. As it is a trifle difficult to split a bridge at a baseboard joint, I suggest that the upper deck is a separate lift-off section that slots in-to place when the baseboards are erected.

Plan 40c
Warleggan

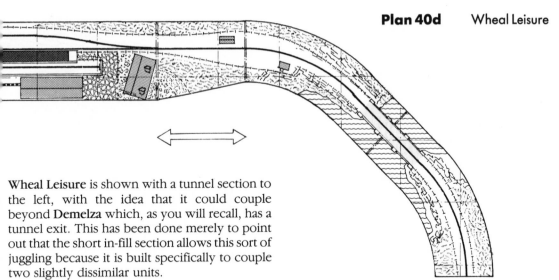

Plan 40d   Wheal Leisure

Wheal Leisure is shown with a tunnel section to the left, with the idea that it could couple beyond **Demelza** which, as you will recall, has a tunnel exit. This has been done merely to point out that the short in-fill section allows this sort of juggling because it is built specifically to couple two slightly dissimilar units.

All the main sections are shown as pairs of mirror image baseboards — most of them are plain rectangles. This is for storage, which is extremely important with this approach. I envisage a steady flow of different stations being built, which means that most must be put away in the loft, ideally cocooned in plastic sheeting fixed to the framing with a staple gun or stuck down with wide sticky tape. The fill-in sections are more difficult, since each is a different size and shape. Here I suggest you first obtain a stout carton of convenient size and make the fill-in section to fit. You will probably need to put some packing in to hold it securely. Expanded polystyrene blocks, the sort that are thrown away in quantity by electrical retailers, are ideal as they are both strong and light.

I have taken the station names from the 'Poldark' novels. Winston Graham found both **Warleggan** and **Demelza** on Cornish signposts, so I have merely given **Poldark** a location. Come to think of it, Verity would be a good name for the next section.

Plan No. 41a   Creytun (1)
EM gauge 3.10 m × 0.44 m; Steam motive power; **Country of origin** Britain; **Other recommended gauges** OO, P4, HO, N; **Minimum radius** 1,000 mm; **Train length** 4 coaches; Medium points; Turn-of-the-century terminus capable of easy expansion.

Almost all of these plans have been preceded by a number of rough pencil sketches, usually on the back of a piece of scrap A4 paper (the traditional back of an envelope, I find, is totally inadequate). With this preparation I usually can go straight ahead and produce the finished plan, but **Creytun** was the exception. Two detailed outlines had to be abandoned in favour of the one you see before you. The sectional nature of a portable scheme permits one to build a fairly large station to a high level of craftsmanship without spending years before you reach the point where the model looks reasonably finished and is capable of decent operation.

I envisaged a turn-of-the-century setting and wanted a fairly impressive small double-track terminus, where prototype-length trains could be run. It was clear that this would be a long-term project since, in addition to the layout itself, most if not all of the locomotives and rolling stock must be either kit-built or scratchbuilt. So Plan No. 41a on three short baseboards provides a minimal operating layout. Goods facilities are a little meagre and there is no goods shed as such, so initially you could install one in place of the small factory close to the over-bridge. The layout lacks locomotive facilities as well, and whilst operable, is a trifle limited in all directions.

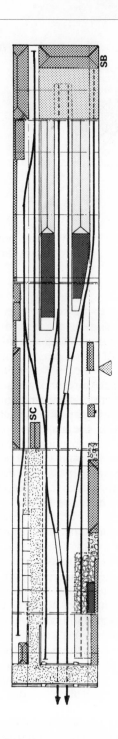

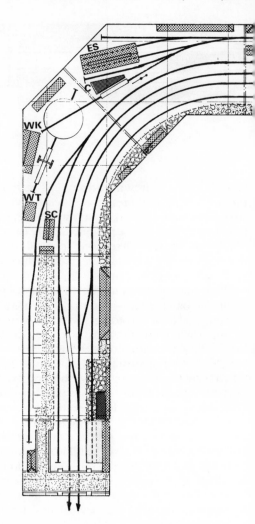

Plan 41a   Creytun (1)

Plan No. 41b   Creytun (2)

EM gauge 3.70 m × 2.25 m; Steam motive power; **Country of origin** Britain; **Other recommended gauges** OO, HO, N; **Minimum radius** 700 mm; **Train length** 5 coaches; Scratchbuilt points; Final form of extensible turn-of-the-century layout.

This does not matter, since in Plan No. 41b these deficiencies are overcome. A large curved section holds the locomotive depot and also gives an effective run round loop clear of the platform roads. In view of the separation of the final turnouts from the station proper, a further signal

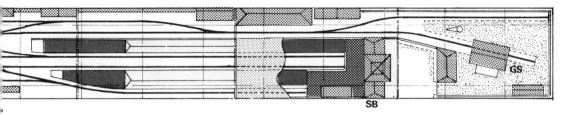

Plan 41b   Creytun (2)

cabin is provided because mechanical operation would not stretch as far as this.

The locomotive depot is fairly typical of a small mid-Victorian installation, complete with a small repair shop with sheer-legs over the cripple road. Although only two locomotives can be put in the shed, four to six would be allocated to this depot and would stand out overnight on various spurs by the shed.

At the other end of the layout, two new boards not only provide a modest goods yard, complete with shed and offices, but also extend the station to take five coaches, six at a pinch, since early bogie stock was appreciably shorter than the modern coach I normally specify. I suggest a fairly well-developed concourse together with an impressive main station building overlooking a small station yard. The initial station building is replaced, but not scrapped, as it could well be that this extended system can only be conveniently erected at exhibitions.

I have mentioned exhibition use throughout, since one advantage of the truly portable layout is that it can be easily taken to a show. At least it is supposed to be an advantage, but if a layout becomes popular, the owner will find a lot of his weekends and part of his annual leave bespoke. This is a matter for personal decision, but there is one vital point to mention. Only accept invitations where the organizers offer decent expenses, a mileage allowance rather than just petrol costs, meals for you and your relief operator(s), and insurance to cover fully the layout to and from the show as well as during the entire opening. In the case of a charity show you can waive expenses, and you would probably do so for your own club, but adequate insurance is a rock-bottom essential. Do not undervalue your work. A simple working layout is worth several hundred pounds, and some of the designs in this book should, if properly built, be valued in thousands. A kit-built locomotive is worth at least £80, more likely double this, whilst a fine scratchbuilt model would be realistically valued at something approaching a thousand pounds. If you do not believe me, just check the prices reached at auction, or charged by professional modelmakers.

CHAPTER 9

Something in the city

Model railways are inevitably built in cramped situations, where one has perforce to squeeze the essential facilities into the smallest possible space. It is all too common under such circumstances to select a country branch prototype, and agreed, the simple track plans can be compressed to half their length without any real loss of character, whilst a two-coach train is perfectly acceptable. However, the fact is that the overwhelming majority of country stations sprawl all over the place, for the simple reason that when they were built land was cheap and, having learned their lesson the hard way, the planners left ample space for later expansion — which rarely, if ever, occurred.

City stations, on the other hand, are built on cramped sites, since land is expensive and, in general, insufficient was bought initially to accommodate the inevitable expansion. So such stations are really much better choices for the modeller who has a modest amount of space to hand. There is the added bonus that the largest and most prestigious locomotives are no longer out of place.

Plan No. 42   Dugdale Road
OO gauge 3.75 m × 0.28 m; Open motive power; **Country of origin** Britain; **Other recommended gauges** O, HO, EM/P4, N; **Minimum radius** 1,000 mm; **Train length** 3 coaches; Medium points; Expandable single-track city terminus.

It was with this in mind that I produced Plan No. 42. The need was urgent: my eldest son had learned that a former undergraduate at Bristol University once had a 009 layout in his room at Hall. Family honour was at stake, we had to devise a main line OO gauge layout that could also fit into a student's room. **Dugdale Road** was the result.

Plan 42   Dugdale Road

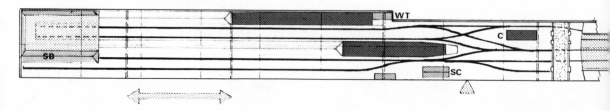

The original model opened up to 10 ft in length, and closed down to 2 ft 6 in to go into a cupboard. This was a little restrictive and so the layout has been rebuilt much as shown here, and, in its fully extended form, the model will take a seven-car Western Region HST. The section of baseboard marked with the shaded arrow is optional, and only used for exhibition purposes where a much larger fiddle yard is employed. Although I envisaged steam operation, Nick sensibly follows modern practice, basing his stock mainly on the locomotives he saw in Bristol during his studies.

Operation is interesting. The line is single track, entry and exit being made along the central road. The lower road, in imagination, leads to the goods yard, whilst the upper runs to the locomotive depot. The fiddle yard on **Dugdale Road** works overtime!

The layout is much more effective as a diesel era model, since the freight services are all block trains and naturally do not need a brake van, which simplifies shunting. Not that there is a lot of simplification in this area, since the layout requires two station pilots, whilst the platform roads are electrically sub-divided so that DMUs can be joined or split.

In the ten years since it was built, Dugdale Road has had its trackage increased by some 200 per cent without the addition of a single point. The track is beginning to show its age and although it is likely that any successor will have a double track exit, the basic layout may well be copied.

Plan No. 43   Crutched Friars

OO gauge 3.10 m × 0.36 m; Open motive power; **Country of origin** Britain; **Other recommended gauges** O, HO, EM/P4, N; **Minimum radius** 1,000 mm; **Train length** 5 coaches; Medium points; City terminus for passenger and van traffic only.

In **Crutched Friars**, Plan No. 43, we have a four platform terminus where the roads are of two different lengths, allowing space for a complete model of the station building to be included within the platform width. This breaks the station into the main and local roads, while the overall roof is shown as a pair of pitched roofs. It

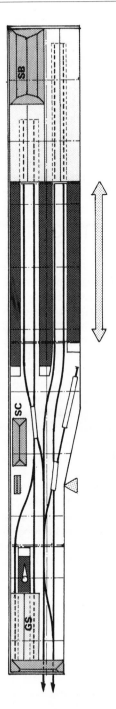

Plan 43   Crutched Friars

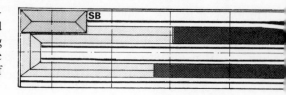

could be constructed from any of the commercial roofing kits, some adjustment in baseboard dimensions being made to fit. By incorporating two double slips we not only save space, but we also increase the appearance of complexity of the station throat.

The two shortened platform roads allow room for a respectably sized station building, and force the use of twin overall roofs. As should by now be fairly obvious, I like this feature. It is impressive and yet a lot easier to arrange than a set of umbrella roofs over the platforms. Furthermore, since the roof can be easily lifted off, access to the tracks during operation is quite simple.

The freight facilities are clearly geared for van traffic, and are none the worse for this. Now that a wide selection of vans is available, this option is one that ought to be fully exploited.

A token goods shed is provided, which I suggest would handle van traffic rather than general merchandise. I have shown the exit under a large building, which would be carried over the track on a heavy plate girder. This is typical of many city sites, where even the space over the railway has a high enough value to warrant the cost of bridging. Today, it is not uncommon to provide a raft over the entire station area, supporting a shopping centre and a large office block, but while this would certainly produce an unsual model, it would hardly be a convenient one!

As before, there is a filler section extending the platform length. I'm assuming that whilst few modellers would have room to accommodate a full–length station, a cut down version for home use, with provision for extension at exhibitions is perfectly acceptable. However, as omitting the complete unit would not only eliminate the two shorter local platforms, but also make it virtually impossible to shunt the goods shed, I would advise a shorter insert, something between 200 and 300 mm in length.

Plan No. 44 Banwell
OO gauge 4.50 m × 0.63 m; Steam motive power; **Country of origin** Britain; **Other recommended gauges** O, HO, EM/P4, N; **Minimum radius** 1,000 mm; **Train length** 4 coaches; Large points; Main line terminus based on Bill Banwell and Frank Applegate's *Maybank*.

Plan No. 44 is based loosely on the first practical terminus-fiddle yard scheme to be exhibited, **Maybank**. I have followed the general plan, a double track terminus with minimal goods facilities, with a rising track to the locomotive shed above the fiddle yard. The details, however, differ considerably.

Due to lack of space, the signal cabin is an overtrack pattern, used on the prototype where there was no room for a conventional ground level box either. In model form this can be very convenient, as the signals can be placed on short dolls directly outside the box, and with ample room inside for electromagnets operation is fairly straightforward.

I assume that **Banwell** would be erected along one side of a garage. It would need to be fairly high to clear the side of the car — the tumblehome of a modern saloon makes this feasible, but it would be more convenient were the garage some 300 mm wider than usual. I am not dwelling deeply on this layout, since if one can take over the whole of the garage, a much better arrangement is possible and this is dealt with later in this book.

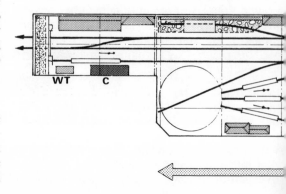

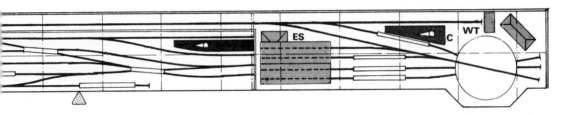

Plan 44   Banwell

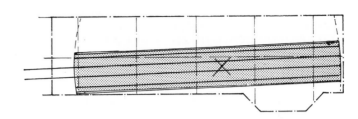

Banwell is essentially an operating layout, with only minimal scenic development, as was the case on the original. Here, without a doubt, the trains are the main attraction.

Plan No. 45   Avon
OO gauge 4.38 m × 0.57 m; Steam motive power; **Country of origin** Britain; **Other recommended gauges** O, EM/P4, HO, N; **Minimum radius** 1,000 mm; **Train length** 5 coaches; Large points; Portable city terminus layout, expandable for exhibition.

Avon has a number of interesting features. As with **Crutched Friars**, this layout can be ap-

preciably shortened by omitting the optional section, a feature which can be very useful in the home environment when the short platforms would be reduced to short loading bays for parcels traffic.

Avon provides a reasonable goods yard, whilst still allowing three platform roads. There are two optional sections, one to lengthen the platform faces, one to provide a turntable together with locomotive lie-by roads. This arrangement is inspired by the old Ranelagh depot at Paddington.

Shunting must perforce take place on the main line, but this was not entirely unknown on the

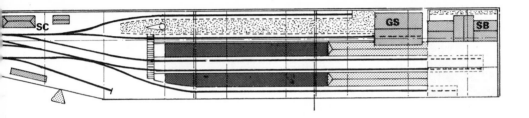

Plan 45   Avon

prototype in such situations. Clearly, it would take place outside the rush hour and be a very deliberate business under the direct control of the signalman. You will note that I have shown umbrella roofs in addition to the main overall span. These are an optional extra on all large stations that can be erected during the later developments.

Plan No. 46 Bishopsgate

OO gauge 2.40 m × 0.35 m; Steam motive power; **Country of origin** Britain (London); **Other recommended gauges** O, EM/P4, HO, N; **Minimum radius** 1,000 mm; **Train length** 4 coaches; Large points; Based on Metropolitan Railway prototype in 1890s.

Plan No. 46 is a conjectural reconstruction of **Bishopsgate**, Metropolitan Railway in steam days, when the link into Liverpool Street was still in use. Details of the station are alas, very vague. All I know is that the platforms were shorter than those at the modern Liverpool Street, and there was an overall roof, presumably similar to the one at Paddington (Circle Line), in place of the present block of offices and shops. Furthermore, that slip ought by rights to be a single slip, but I have indulged in a little modellers' licence to allow for more complicated working.

   The lines shown are suggested for exhibition use, and demonstrate how easily one can produce a layout where over 60 per cent of the tracks are 'off–stage'. Three fiddle yards could be employed to considerable advantage. The station may be worked as a terminus, which is why we have that double slip. I would also suggest further use of modellers' licence so that a wide selection of London-based suburban tank locomotives, with appropriate stock, could be built, begged or borrowed, using the station as an authentic background for a parade of stock around the turn of the century. Liverpool St (Met), to give the prototype its later name, is of particular interest since I had this station in mind when I began the doodle that ended up as Minories, one of the most popular layouts I have ever designed.

Plan 46   Bishopsgate

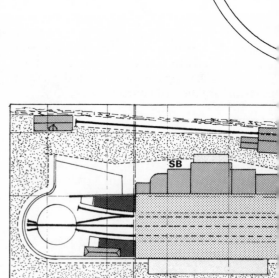

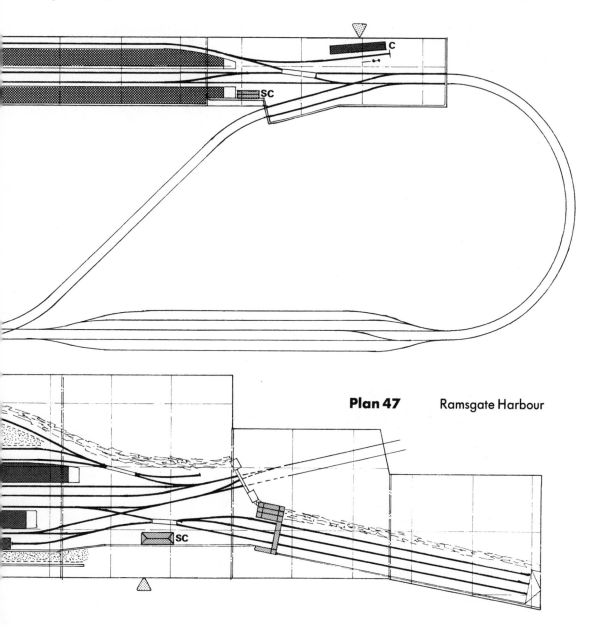

Plan 47   Ramsgate Harbour

Plan No. 47   Ramsgate Harbour
EM/P4 gauge 4.425 m × 1.125 m; Steam motive power; **Country of origin** Britain (Kent); **Other recommended gauges** OO, HO, N; **Minimum radius** 1,000 mm; **Train length** 7 coaches; Scratchbuilt points; Based on LCDR prototype, ca 1925.

Although Ramsgate is not strictly speaking a city, the old harbour station of the LCDR was in a very confined site and, as Plan No. 47 shows, it can be a very effective prototype. I am indebted to Malcolm Parker, who provided the original sketch from which the plan is drawn, but who is not responsible for the fact that, I have reduced the model in length by some 600 mm. I may well have inadvertently made a couple of other slight alterations in order to fit it comfortably on to sectional baseboards, but the end result appears authentic enough.

The prototype was worked with arrival (seaward) and departure (cliff) platforms and would be extremely difficult to work in any other way! There was a lot of shunting, much of it inside the inclined tunnel. The turntable provided for locomotive release was 50 ft in diameter, considerably smaller than I normally draw on a model, but it did handle the 4-4-0s that worked the line in later days.

The plan shows the track arrangement in the early 'twenties, just before closure. Although this took place whilst I was still an infant, I have visited the site when it was an amusement arcade. The setting is excellent, and in place of the usual backscene you have a 20 m high chalk cliff. This would make working a fiddle yard a trifle fraught, or else block out the view of the trains if you were to operate from the other side, though this would be the obvious arrangement for an exhibition. I have therefore suggested how **Ramsgate Harbour** could be arranged in a fairly large space, such as a loft. It is a very practical layout, and in deference to Malcolm's own unfinished essay, before he changed to 7 mm scale, I have suggested it should be P4 rather than EM or OO.

Plan No. 48a Hungerford Bridge

EM gauge 4.20 m × 0.60 m; Open motive power; **Country of origin** Britain (London);

Other recommended gauges OO, HO, N; **Minimum radius** 1,000 mm; **Train length** 7 coaches; Large points; High level city terminus with river bridge access.

The Southern theme is continued in the last of our city stations. The suggested name for Plan No. 48a shows what I had in mind, but only the setting is reminiscent of Charing Cross.

Hungerford Bridge is getting close to the limit for a single–handed enthusiast, and would best be constructed by a small syndicate, one of whom must like modelling intricate girderwork! Whilst not out of place in the home, though its length could be a little bit of a problem, it is really intended for exhibition, where two extra sections, lengthening the platforms and the bridge, could well be added. I have also shown a suggested plan for an add-on station building and forecourt, assuming, with some justification, that any modelling syndicate will have in its number one or two modellers who enjoy making challenging buildings.

The third track on the bridge would, as on the prototype-once-removed, be mainly used as a carriage siding and, if steam working were the rule, as a run-round loop. There is another carriage storage road between the two main platforms whilst a short bay road, which will probably act as a locomotive refuge, is between the two pairs of platforms.

The main road looks rather like the Embankment, and indeed that is what I had in mind. I have shown it in its modern dual carriageway form, since the original arrangement, with the conduit trams, could lead to even more com-

Plan 48a   Hungerford Bridge

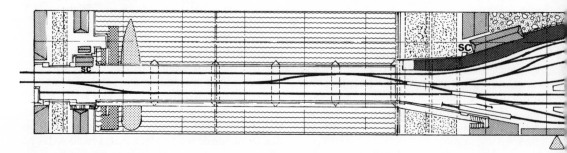

plications if someone decided to make them work! There is, in addition, a central cab road leading up from a street passing under the station. Indeed a long road linking the forecourt with the Embankment could be added, I am assuming, of course, that once those structure modellers get the bit between their teeth, there will be no stopping them.

Personally, I would love to see this layout built with steam and electric stock, either in the late 1930s or the early post-war period. The line needs no backscene as such and is equally attractive from either side, so there is no need to swap the operating position for exhibition use.

Plan No. 48b Basin Street
EM gauge 3.60 m × 0.75 m; Open motive power; **Country of origin** Britain (London); **Other recommended gauges** OO, HO, N; **Minimum radius** 700 mm; **Train length** 12 coaches; Medium points; Loco depot and main line loops for Hungerford Bridge.

For the track builders, an even more ambitious exhibition extra is possible. Plan No. 48b, **Basin Street**, not only provides a small locomotive depot, inspired by but not based on Ewer Street, but also adds a junction that allows proper out-and-back working and provides more scope for the building workers. This layout is designed to fit on a reasonably–sized baseboard and could be slightly enlarged and split over two sections to advantage. Even though I feel that, in its fully extended form, this project is one for a specialist section of a large model railway club, with commodious clubrooms, it is still best to keep the

sections small, since this makes the trip to exhibitions much easier. Far better to put the team to work erecting the units than to insist that at least two members are needed to carry each section. Although access to exhibition halls is easy, with wide doors and passageways, there is almost invariably a good deal of manhandling involved between the place you have parked the van and the ultimate location of the layout. It is bad enough having to hump about a large layout to set it up, but it can prove to be the proverbial last straw at the end of a long show.

It might be thought that, with this layout fully extended, few if any exhibition managers would look on it favourably. I doubt that this would be a problem, because providing the model were built to current state-of-the-art standards, either in EM or P4, and initially shown in its shorter form, it would be a very popular crowd-puller. Something along these lines would do wonders for the Southern railway, or Southern region, not to mention EMU modelling. Overall I think the third rail is a must.

Before I leave the scheme, I should add that Glasgow also has a large river, and that there are several railway bridges across the Clyde, so the London setting is not essential. I know and love Glasgow Central, but I know London far better. I am, after all, a cockney.

Throughout this chapter, I have considered 4 mm scale, British practice. Needless to say, Continental HO is equally applicable to city schemes, though if German or Austrian prototypes were favoured, the models should be built as mirror images. In point of fact, the initial idea for

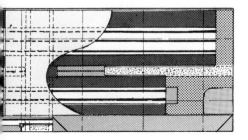

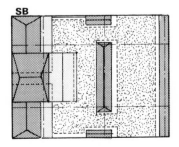

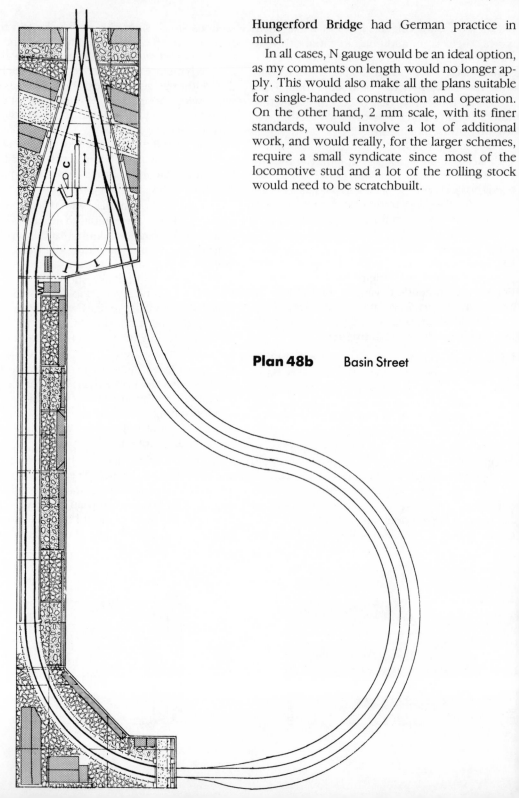

Hungerford Bridge had German practice in mind.

In all cases, N gauge would be an ideal option, as my comments on length would no longer apply. This would also make all the plans suitable for single-handed construction and operation. On the other hand, 2 mm scale, with its finer standards, would involve a lot of additional work, and would really, for the larger schemes, require a small syndicate since most of the locomotive stud and a lot of the rolling stock would need to be scratchbuilt.

Plan 48b   Basin Street

CHAPTER 10

The railway room

There is little doubt that far and away the best arrangement is for a model railway to be housed in a room where it has priority. When this can be contrived without any risk of the space being needed for some other purpose, it is to be recommended. However even where the room may be required for some other purpose on a temporary basis, it is still a good idea, providing the layout is made on sectioned bases so it can be dismantled and stored, probably in the loft, and subsequently re-erected.

It is often suggested that a permanent layout should always be built in sections, so that in the event of a move, the model can be easily re-erected in its new home. This is utter nonsense. In the course of several moves I have never found this to be possible, for the new site is always quite different and the layout can only be fitted in after major surgery, which all too often fails to produce a decent model. Where frequent moves are probable, a portable scheme, which fits very loosely into any likely site, is the best arrangement.

Apart from this, a permanent layout is more conveniently constructed on an open-top framing, even where a single level scheme is contemplated. However, as a quick flip through this section shows, another advantage of a permanent site is that multi-level schemes can be tackled with confidence. In addition, one can curve the front fascia of the baseboard to provide a visually attractive 'soft edge' to the model.

Plan No. 49 Wrangton
OO gauge 2.40 m × 1.95 m; Steam motive power; **Country of origin** Britain; **Other recommended gauges** HO, N*; **Minimum radius** 600 mm; **Train length** 4 coaches; Medium points; Point to point, single-track system.

As with most projects, a permanent layout is best begun at the bottom so I shall describe **Wrangton**, a simple single–track branch scheme, in this order. We start with a turntable pattern fiddle yard tucked in the corner beside the doorway. This is the most practical form of reversing arrangement where the yard is below baseboard level, since the clearance available is rather too small to allow one to see the trains, let alone handle them! From here the line climbs steadily, emerging from a tunnel to reach a tiny halt which as shown is only capable of handling single coach trains. This is little more than a scenic feature and as such is capable of considerable modification to suit your taste.

The line then dives under the terminus **Wrangton**, to emerge on to the lift-out section, which I have suggested takes the form of a three-arch bridge over a small valley. With a 6 mm thick plywood track base and 6 mm ply profiled sides, secured to two 12 mm thick ply or timber end pieces, cross-braced with four 20 × 12 mm timber piers, one gets a strong, yet light structure.

We now reach the passing station. I am assum-

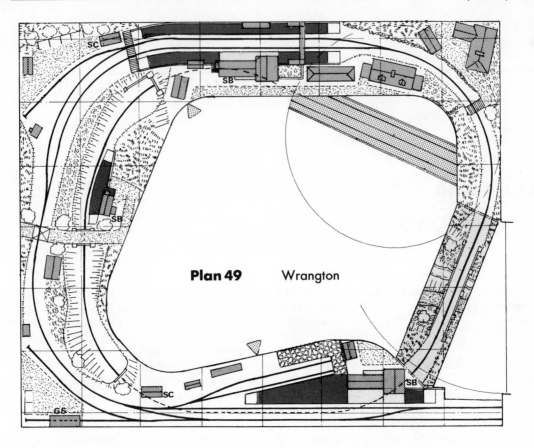

Plan 49   Wrangton

ing that there will normally be just the one operator, and so it is extremely simple in design, making remote control from the main panel a straightforward option. It is well developed scenically, with enough buildings scattered around to suggest that a small hamlet has grown around the station, which, as was commonplace on the old country railway, is some distance from the main village. This is one reason why the railway succumbed to the bus, which in turn is losing ground to the private car.

The terminus is unconventional in model terms, though not all that unusual on the prototype, in that the platform does not reach the end of the line. This is partly because the door is shown very close to the side wall, a very common arrangement in small rooms. Operationally, this arrangement is more convenient since the arriving locomotive will then stand convenient-

ly beyond the far end of the platform road. If a little more width is available a locomotive coaling stage and water column would be an interesting addition.

A more important feature is that the various sidings are scattered about the station, leading to some rather complicated moves when marshalling a freight train. This adds operating interest to what is, perforce, a fairly simple station.

Plan No. 50   Vennburgh
OO gauge 2.10 m × 2.025 m; Steam motive power; **Country of origin** Britain; **Other recommended gauges** HO, N*; **Minimum radius** 600 mm; **Train length** 3 coaches; Medium points; Point-to-point, single-track system.

The next layout, Plan No. 50, is a single-track point-to-point system, a type of layout that has, a little unjustly, I feel, fallen out of fashion of late.

Starting at the bottom once again, we have a very simple terminus with the bare minimum of facilities. This gives one clear advantage: you can fit a temporary sector plate fiddle yard at the far side of the room and enjoy operation at a very early stage in the proceedings. The goods yard is rather small and partially located underneath the bridge.

The line begins to climb just outside the lower terminus, passing under the upper station to emerge on to the lift-out section. It then crosses the outer end of the low level terminus on a girder bridge which should be made removable for access and maintenance.

We now reach the main station, **Vennburgh**, an impressive three platform terminus. As the run-round loop is clear of the platforms, these will double as carriage sidings, providing much needed storage space. A separate spur allows locomotives to back into the small depot which, I suggest, is best raised between 9 and 12 mm above the main baseboard, thus providing an interesting variation in levels. This is easily done by simply building it on a separate sheet of board which lies on top of the main base. The goods shed is modelled in partial relief, suggesting it is much larger than it really is. Once again we have the run-round loop on the curve, outside the platform roads, which double as storage sidings. This, incidentally, used to be prototype practice. The early train sheds were provided as much to shelter the stock as to coddle the passengers.

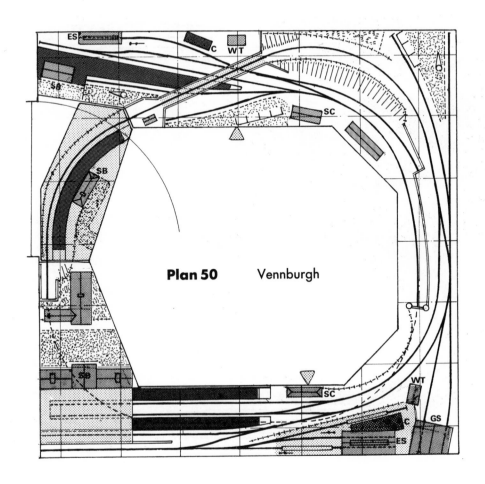

Plan 50   Vennburgh

Plan No. 51   Chapel Meadow

OO gauge 2.85 m × 2.05 m; Open motive power; **Country of origin** Britain (Avon); **Other recommended gauges** HO, N*; **Minimum radius** 600 mm; **Train length** 4 coaches; Medium points; Through terminus with reverse loop; Temple Meads plan.

In Plan No. 51 we come to one of my favourite themes, a through terminus tucked neatly into a corner, and inspired by Temple Meads, Bristol. **Chapel Meadow** is a fairly conventional out-and-back system with continuous run scheme but calls for a little careful planning if the gradients are not to be too severe. If we take the loop under the main station as the datum level, the passing station should be at mid-level whilst the main station is, obviously, at summit level. As one needs some 75 mm clearance for OO, plus at least 12 mm for the thickness of the sub-base, the line needs to climb a minimum of 87 mm, say 100 mm for comfort, so a ruling gradient of around 1 in 40 is indicated.

There are two obvious lift-out sections, the lines across the doorway and the return from the loop which breaks the main operating and viewing well into two sections. I also suggest that the goods yard is arranged to lift off so that not only can you build the main station complex, but you can also subsequently reach the tracks for maintenance.

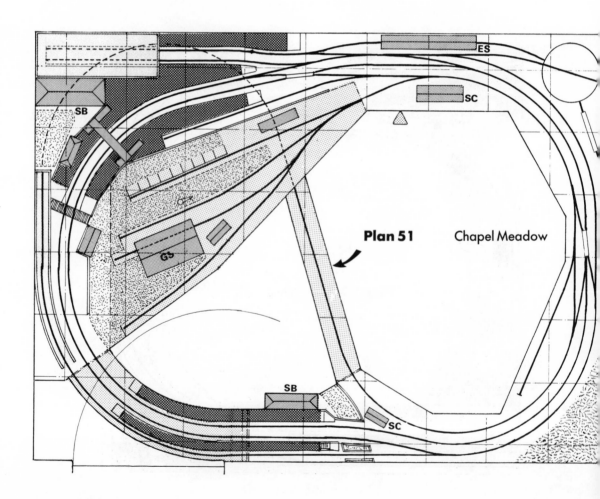

Plan 51   Chapel Meadow

Plan 52   Fore Street

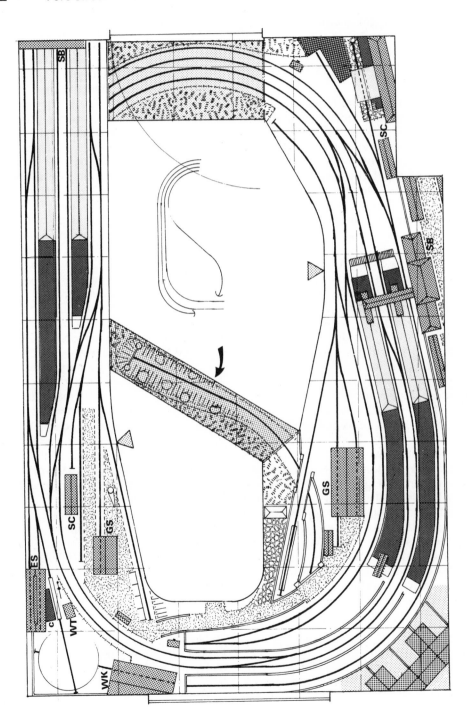

Plan No. 52   Fore Street

OO gauge 3.15 m × 2.1 m; Steam motive power; **Country of origin** Britain; **Other recommended gauges** EM, HO, N*; **Minimum radius** 600 mm; **Train length** 6 coaches; Medium points; Out-and-back layout with quadruple track effect.

As I have mentioned before, I consider that for single–handed operation, the terminus-reverse loop out-and-back scheme is easily the best possible arrangement and in Plan No. 52 I provide another version of one of my favourite schemes. **Fore Street** has a large four-platform terminus at high level, with a decent-sized goods yard. The modest locomotive depot has a spur off the turntable running into a small locomotive maintenance building, and the goods yard has three sidings, with the short spur provided to hold the brake vans during re-marshalling.

The line then falls to enter the centre roads of an impressive four-road through station and proceeds, after a short level section through the platforms, to fall further as it joins the quadruple track and passes over the main lift-out section to dive beneath the terminus. The inset sketch shows the arrangement of the hidden tracks. The centre pair climbs around the room to emerge running along the outside of the through platforms. From here, crossovers allow the trains to lap the layout, or to proceed by means of a low-level reverse loop to retrace their journey. We thus have true quadruple track which makes sense, though it is used to extend the length of run. Storage roads off the reverse loops would add to the amount of stock that could be handled, and allow an even better timetable to be devised.

There are reasonable goods facilities at the passing station, and two operators could have a great deal of fun with this model. However, the line can be worked single–handed if desired, since it is not essential to set any of the points at the intermediate station to keep up a normal service.

Plan No. 53   Smeaton

OO/HO gauge 3.00 m × 2.15 m; Steam motive power; **Country of origin** Britain; **Other recommended gauges** HO, N*; **Minimum radius** 600 mm; **Train length** 3 coaches; Medium points; Out-and-back scheme, showing utilization of chimney breast.

Plan No. 53 provides a simple out-and-back double–track layout with a reasonable though by no means elaborate operating potential. There is a good deal of compromise involved: train lengths are short, and one of the three platforms at Smeaton is only able to receive trains, and will probably be of more value as a parcels road and storage siding.

I have included a chimney breast in this scheme just to demonstrate how awkward it can be to make much use of the two alcoves. Indeed, one of them is primarily used for scenic purposes, providing the small yard with a background of warehouses and cattle dock. The second alcove allows for a little more siding space and, once again, gives room to model a small goods yard with all the essential features.

As there is little room for a full locomotive depot at the main station, I have provided two sidings with inspection pits and watering facilities, and set the main depot, with turntable and shed, at the passing station.

The passing station incorporates a terminal bay for local trains. As drawn, the layout implies the last days of steam, with the local services being worked by railcars. However, there is no reason why this should be so, for you can operate a steam-hauled local service using one block set of coaches and a minimum of three suitable tank locomotives. In this case, the railcar shed would be removed and the siding used to hold a spare tank locomotive.

Plan No. 54   Holman Valley

OO gauge 4.00 m × 3.00 m; Steam motive power; **Country of origin** Britain; **Other recommended gauges** EM, HO, N*; **Minimum radius** 500 mm; **Train length** 3 coaches; Small points; Extensive single track system inspired by Col. Stephens' light railway.

So far, I have kept to fairly small rooms, assuming that the larger ones will be needed for normal household purposes. However, if one of the larger rooms can be spared, the possibilities are considerable as we see in Plan No. 54, **Holman**

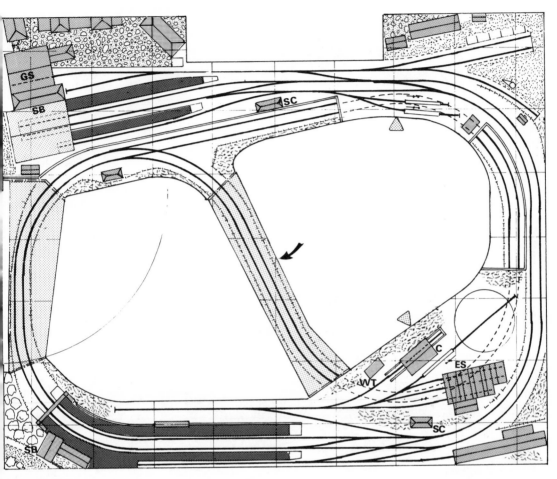

Plan 53   Smeaton

Valley. My inspiration is, in part, the work of the late John H. Ahern with the Madder Valley and, of course, the gloriously eccentric light railways built and run by the late Col. H. F. Stephens. The situation is the English Shires, sometime between the wars, and it is probably high summer.

Starting near the bottom as usual, we find an interchange station built alongside a river. There is a medium sized locomotive shed with a carriage alongside. The locomotive valeting facilities are economically placed on the spur and the station buildings are very plain. Timber construction is, I feel, inevitable. A light bridge across the river leads to a small goods yard, then, as the tracks leave the station, they divide. One

falls fairly rapidly and disappears beneath the only overbridge. An adjacent building suggests it heads off through the wall, but in practice it turns to emerge as a tiny fiddle yard at a low level in front of the high level station. This feature allows one to transfer empty and loaded goods stock to the rest of Britain, but would never be employed for through passenger working. With a Colonel Stephens line you got out and walked; anything under a mile was just around the corner in his way of thinking.

Meantime the main line is climbing before diving into the tunnel. This tunnel is worthy of note, for such arrangements were most unusual on light railways. However, there was one on

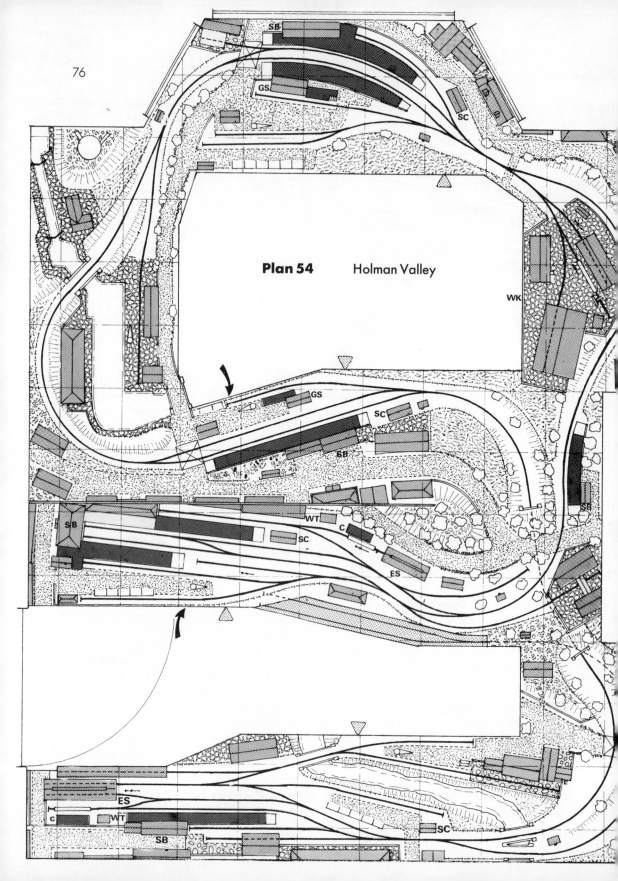

Plan 54   Holman Valley

the East Kent, so, once again, there is prototype justification. Leaving the tunnel, the line emerges at a small station which is not, strictly speaking, a passing station, as the second through road is only a goods loop. There is just the one siding.

The climb continues, the line now curving around a canal basin with a long siding running down to the canal wharf. This rather pleasing scenic feature is, I suggest, crowned by one of the ruins that Cromwell knocked about a bit.

We now enter the main intermediate station, which has a proper passing loop, a fairly extensive goods yard and is close to the railway's workshops. Here there is a smithy, a locomotive erecting shop and a general workshop where the carriages are patched up. Sheer legs span a road in the open.

The line curves behind the shops and comes to a simple halt alongside an ungated level crossing. Then we end the steady climb, which has been punctuated only by the level loops in the two stations, to arrive at the upper terminus.

For once there is a decent brick-built station building. I suggest it began life as a large private house, and now houses the company's offices. We have a platform awning, and a reasonable supply of facilities, for here, with a convenient site near to the cattle market, the light railway is hopefully competing for traffic in what I think is a pleasant, sleepy cathedral city. There is very little traffic anyway, since the Bishop, Dean and Chapter will naturally use the rather less conveniently-reached main line station for their trips to London and the Athenaeum.

With a light railway such as this, the stock would, in the main, consist of second-hand main line equipment, leading to a gloriously heterogenous collection. When John Ahern built the Madder Valley everything had to be scratch-built. Today, in 4 mm scale, there are several suitable ready-to-run locomotives and a plethora of usable kits. An important aspect of the Madder Valley was the lineside buildings and therefore I have shown a large number of them lining the model. Note how the backscene along the central baseboard divides the two stations scenically.

Into the bargain, as the door opens into the main operating well, there is no need for a lift-out section, and access to the space beyond the main station is by crawling under the baseboard. This is not really inconvenient, as you do not need to get there that often, and, as has already been pointed out on many occasions, this does ensure one gets ample exercise! It is possible to operate single-handed, with the passing loops operated by point motors and controlled either locally or from the high level terminus panel. Two operators are best, and up to four can be accommodated.

Plan No. 55   Embury
EM gauge 3.60 m × 3.00 m; Steam motive power; **Country of origin** Britain; **Other recommended gauges** OO, HO, N*; **Minimum radius** 750 mm; **Train length** 4 coaches; Medium points; Urban double-track point-to-point.

Normally one orients the stations on the longer axis of a room, for obvious reasons, but when the short axis is long enough to provide for a reasonable length train, you can gain a great deal from a less conventional approach as I have done in **Holman Valley**. This also allowed me to make good use of the alcoves beside the chimney breast. The same principle is applied to Plan No. 55, **Embury**. In this instance we have a double-track point-to-point which combines a busy track layout, with ample storage facilities, with a very impressive urban scenic development. Once again, the door opens into the main operating well, and one has to duck under to reach the access space by the loops.

Whilst parts of the main station yard, and almost all of the motive power depot, are out of convenient reach, given the prime essentials of well-laid track and properly maintained locomotives and rolling stock, only sheer carelessness will lead to derailments. Hard by the goods shed we have a short spur which is there to hold the brake van whilst shunting, a useful feature on any operational layout. As the yard is some distance from the operator, a reliable auto-coupling is a prime necessity here, but there are several on the market if the trusty Walkley pattern tension lock is not to your taste.

The continuous run emerges in front of the

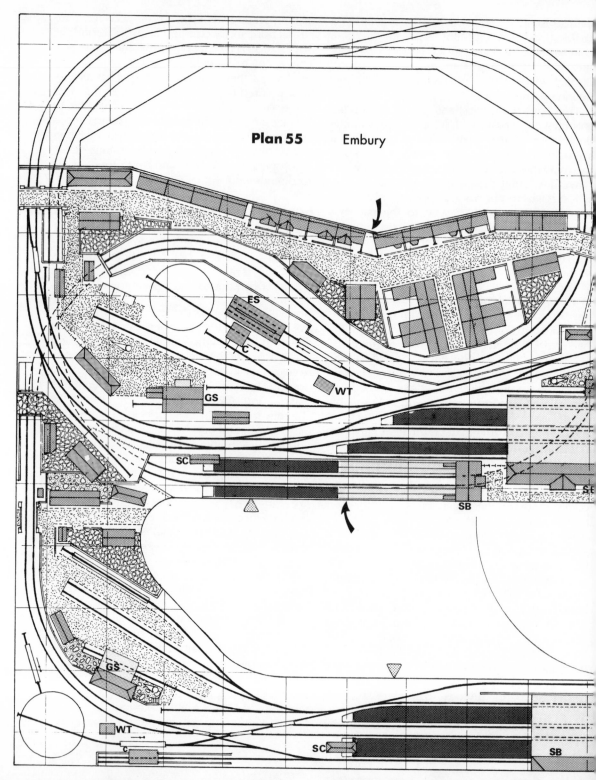

Plan 55 Embury

main station, and has a pair of platforms and nothing else. This not only provides an interesting scenic effect, but also allows one to differentiate operationally between express and local services. I would suggest contrasting architectural styles for the two adjacent station buildings, thus implying that this cheek-by-jowl arrangement occurred when two pre-group companies vied for traffic in the golden days of rail travel.

The low-level terminus is fairly conventional. I have shown another overall roof since this is rather easier to provide than the umbrella roofs that would otherwise be essential. The locomotive facilities are less elaborate, no more than valeting services, and I have also indicated a different type of goods shed, purely to inject a little variety into the scene. There is no reason why you should follow suit, particularly if you are using a commercial kit. Additionally there are very effective coal drops, which lead to still further variation of levels on the model. These are a feature of the design and should be carefully considered before construction begins. Indeed, with this as with many other complicated layouts, a small wood, card and modelling-clay model of the proposed model, at a scale of 1:10 or 1:12 is a very good idea. It is more easily read than a two-dimensional paper plan and the small amount of time involved will be amply repaid during construction.

I have not suggested any storage loops beyond the scenic section, though this useful addition could probably be worked in when the whole thing was laid out to full size. I was more concerned to maintain a slightly larger main line radius with the view to permitting EM gauge if desired. I would hesitate to suggest that P4 is practical in this context, for although some users do claim that 750 mm radius is feasible, the received opinion has it that even 1 m is tight, particularly if large outside cylindered, outside valve-gear steam locomotives are to run over the line. Since the model was designed to allow these magnificent beasts to show their paces in proper form, as I say, I have my doubts.

On one point I have no doubt at all. Although the model can be made with commercial pointwork, the complex station throats would be best scratchbuilt as single units.

CHAPTER 11
The garden shed

The most economical approach to a purpose-built railway room is a small sectional timber shed. However, it is as well to point out that the total cost of fitting out the shed, including a proper damp-proof foundation, an all-weather approach path and, most important of all, the provision of an electricity supply that conforms to regulations, will at least double the cost of a very small shed. It seems from my study of advertisements and garden centres, that shed manufacturers remain wedded to imperial standards and quote sizes in feet. There is an advantage, since 'six by four' trips off the tongue more readily than 'one point eight by one point two'! I will be using the manufacturers' nominal sizes in this chapter, but remember that the quoted sizes are not only nominal but also external, so you do not get a 6 × 4 ft interior. Sheds this size or smaller are really unsuitable for model railways. The smallest practical size is, in my opinion, 7 × 5 ft, which is the subject of Plan No. 56.

Plan No. 56   Edenvale
OO gauge 2.25 m × 1.35 m; Open motive power; **Country of origin** Britain; **Other recommended gauges** O, HO, N*; **Minimum radius** 525 mm; **Train length** 2 coaches; Medium points; Simple continuous run for small shed.

Edenvale is really a scenic test track, just one passing station plus a halt with goods siding, but there is ample room for a modelling workbench beneath the layout. This will make it an ideal test bed for an assiduous kit constructor or scratchbuilder. One of the inherent problems on many large club exhibition layouts is that there is scant opportunity to test the running qualities of the rolling stock before the show and here a layout such as **Edenvale** will prove invaluable. It has enough features set at or near the minimum limits to ensure that the stock is properly checked at home before being taken to the club or exhibition hall.

Plan No. 57   Overton
OO gauge 2.25 m × 1.65 m; Steam motive power; **Country of origin** Britain; **Other recommended gauges** O, HO, N*; **Minimum radius** 600 mm; **Train length** 3 coaches; Medium points; Branch line scheme for small shed.

The slightly larger 8 × 6 ft shed provides better scope and, if the cost of equipping the railway room is borne in mind, is only marginally more expensive than the smaller shed. Plan No. 57 is a variant of one of my favourite themes, a through terminus with curved main line platforms. **Overton** is a development of Plan No. 6, **Zeals**, with larger radii, more facilities in the station and a kickback fiddle yard, which is neatly hidden behind the canal basin. I assume that the canal turns through a right angle after the lock and proceeds across the operating well. It is more

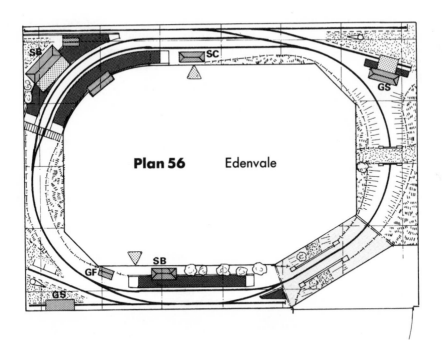

Plan 56 Edenvale

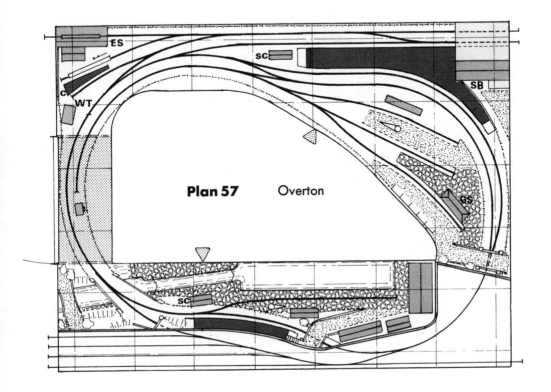

Plan 57 Overton

than just a pleasing scenic feature, for it gives a purpose to the single siding.

You will note that there are several lengths of track projecting outside the main area of the layout. This takes advantage of the fact that a shed has internal timber framing which reduces the internal measurements by roughly 120 mm. However, there is nothing to prevent these tracks being extended into the void, with considerable advantage.

It is very difficult to make any other effective use of this space, but if you set back the backscene behind the overall roof, there would be room for a loading dock. The extra corner could be partially hidden by modelling a warehouse in very low relief at the next set of frames. This sort of treatment is more readily carried out on site than on the drawing board, but the potential does exist and can be exploited to considerable advantage in what is, after all, a very restricted site.

Plan No. 58 Quinton

OO gauge 2.85 m × 2.00 m; Open motive power; **Country of origin** Britain; **Other recommended gauges** HO, N*; **Minimum radius** 600 mm; **Train length** 4 coaches; Medium points; Looped eight plan to fit 10 × 8 shed with extension.

It is also possible to go through a shed's walls. They are, after all, only timber — and fairly thin timber at that! Plan No. 58 forms the familiar looped eight, an arrangement that not only provides a reasonable length of run but also

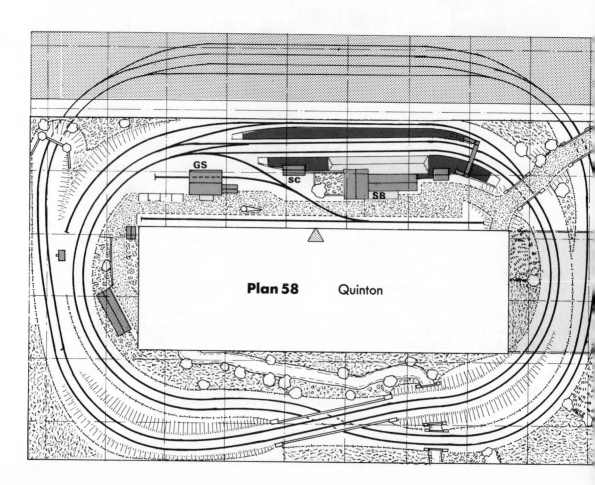

Plan 58   Quinton

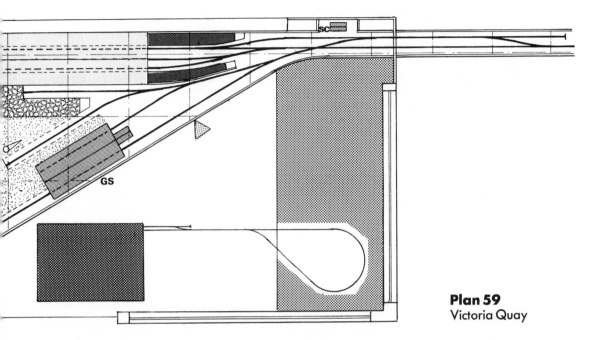

Plan 59
Victoria Quay

produces some effective scenic features. **Quinton** is a fairly conventional passing station with a single loop road and vestigial goods facilities.

The layout is primarily for watching trains go by. It is provided with a set of storage loops outside the shed which I suggest should be housed in a watertight box provided with lifting lids. Needless to say, it is absolutely essential to provide some form of train detection here so that the operator knows whether a particular loop is occupied or not. This arrangement is more accessible than the more conventional method of placing the loops beneath the station, and even though it appears to involve more work, it actually poses fewer constructional problems. It also increases the capacity of the shed for a relatively modest outlay.

Plan No. 59 Victoria Quay
EM gauge 3.00 m × 1.00 m; Steam motive power; **Country of origin** Britain; **Other recommended gauges** OO, HO, N; **Minimum radius** 1,000 mm; **Train length** 4 coaches; Scratchbuilt points; 7 × 5 housing terminus based loosely on Penzance c. 1890, into garden.

Victoria Quay is the final shed scheme and takes the main line out into the garden, the inset sketch showing the simplest possible arrangement. There is nothing to prevent you snaking the tracks all around the garden except, perhaps, opposition from other members of the family.

With a respectable area available for a workbench, this arrangement would suit a scratchbuilder and so I suggest that EM would be possible. OO gauge has been run out of doors for many years, so providing that the outdoor tracks were robust — I would advise PCB-soldered construction — there should be little difficulty. I also make all the outdoor sections as bolt-together frames so that the whole could be dismantled over the winter. I have slight doubts as to the feasibility of P4 out amongst the elements, but if you feel adventurous...

The track layout of **Victoria Quay** is closely based on a photograph of Penzance *circa* 1890, which appears in David St John Thomas's *Great Way West* (David & Charles). The goods layout is conjectural and I have made a small modification to the pointwork at the platform roads, since the prototype had a more complex approach than indicated on my plan. Needless to say, the original was mixed gauge, but I suggest standard gauge, since the prototype was distinctly unusual, a standard gauge outpost linked to the rest of Britain by a linking broad gauge line. The majority of broad gauge locomotives never got that far west and the standard gauge stock was rather bizarre and largely undocumented.

Victoria Quay is a typical late Victorian terminus and although I have quoted four bogie coaches, with 4-wheel and 6-wheel stock, the nominal capacity is greater. The photograph I mention is worth looking up for the general atmosphere of the model, since all that remains today is the magnificent timber roof. In order to accommodate some of the features, notably the signal cabin, I have positioned the backscene behind the line of the internal framing as mentioned in connection with the previous plan.

The garden shed has a good deal going for it, but it does tend to be on the small side. In the next chapter I shall explore the most exciting location to be found in the normal home.

CHAPTER 12
Utilizing the garage

The garage is the largest readily-available space in the home. Agreed, it is there to house the car, even though, in many cases, it is so full of junk the car must perforce stand on the drive. Under such circumstances, it makes sense to throw out the junk and fill the space with a model railway, always remembering that there is a good deal of useful storage space under the baseboard.

However, before we take such a drastic step, there are ways of getting a car to co-exist with a layout. One is a suspended baseboard, which is lifted to the ceiling when not in use. Although this idea has been proposed and even applied to living rooms and bedrooms, I cannot advise too strongly against this. It is all too easy for a rope to break and the whole model to come tumbling down. If it falls on a car, the damage is repairable; if it falls on a member of the family, the result could be fatal. Furthermore, in a garage it is feasible to arrange for lift-out cross-beams which fit into high or low sockets on the walls, thus providing a safe housing at both storage and operating levels.

Plan No. 60 Bruddersford
OO gauge 3.00 m × 2.10 m; Open motive power; Country of origin Britain; Other recommended gauges HO, N*; Minimum radius 600 mm; Train length 4 coaches; Medium points; Lifting double-track point-to-point layout for garage.

Plan No. 60 shows a possible plan for a suspended layout inside a garage, providing an interesting point-to-point double-track layout. It is some 0.6 m smaller than the smallest standard garage, and so there would be very little room around the perimeter for maintenance, but providing the deeper section was placed towards the main door, it would be easy to reach everything from inside. There is nothing particularly novel about **Bruddersford**. The high level terminus has two long and one short platform face, the low level station one main and one bay, with a less elaborate locomotive depot. The intermediate station has four roads to allow expresses to overtake stopping trains, and freight trains to be by-passed. Needless to say, the layout is equally applicable to a room of roughly this size, though some modification to provide access would be advisable in this case.

Plan No. 61 Engandin Sud
HOm gauge 4.50 m × 2.40 m; Electric motive power; Country of origin Switzerland; Other recommended gauges OOn3, HOn3; Minimum radius 360 mm; Train length 6 coaches; Medium points; RhB metre gauge system housed in garage with clearance for car.

Another possibility is to raise the baseboards high enough to allow the car to pass underneath, for the modern car seems to be getting lower and lower. In Plan No. 61 I show a very practical scheme, with a wide array of loops across the

Plan 61
Engandin Sud

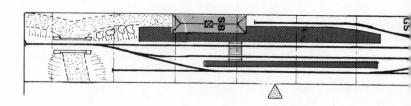

back of the garage, high enough to clear the bonnet, with a relatively narrow baseboard along the left–hand side, allowing easy exit from the car on the right. Indeed, with a Mini the car would fit comfortably outside the layout area.

Engandin Sud is a prototypical 'might-have-been'. There was a proposal to build a line south from Zernez in Switzerland on the Rhaetian

railway's line to Scuol, but as with other planned extensions to the metre gauge, this proposal was abandoned due to the First World War.

The model has the terminus at the summit of the line, something well removed from the actual proposal. The station is laid out as if for future extension, the idea being that the line never got further than this. The through station

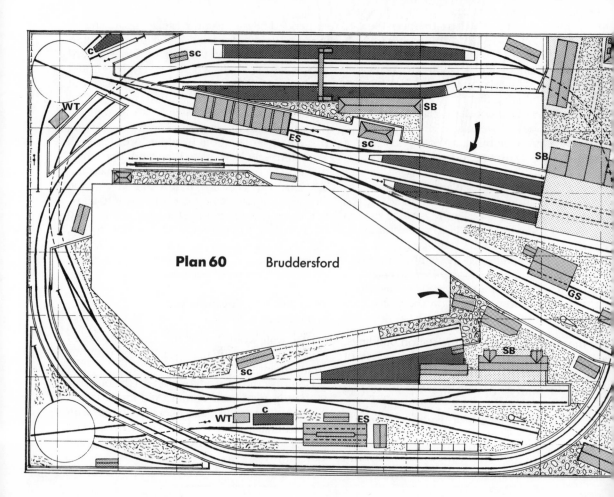

Plan 60   Bruddersford

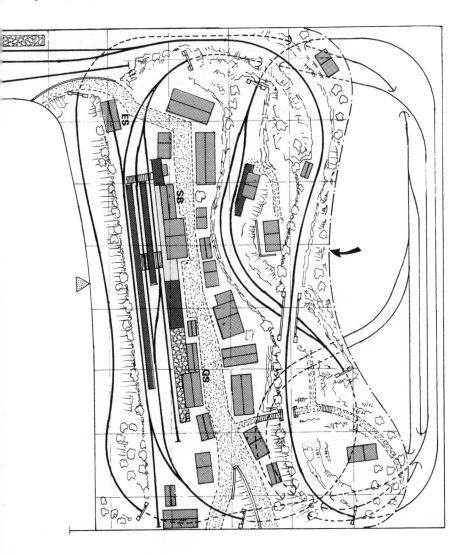

has the goods loop nearest the station buildings, a small factory spur that would be bereft of overhead wires and a small shed at the far end for the diesel tractor which shunts the goods wagons. Yes, that does happen on the RhB.

The line loops its way up the mountain from the base reverse loop, though it does not quite conform to the left-to-right pattern of the prototype's loops. The rear of the baseboard proper ends with the foothills, the backscene on the far wall would show the Alps. One could have a lot of fun with theatrical lighting with this arrangement.

Don't ask me how anyone gets to the building in the top right-hand corner. All I know is that Swiss mountainsides are liberally dotted with isolated chalets that appear to have no contact with the outside world, let alone the road system!

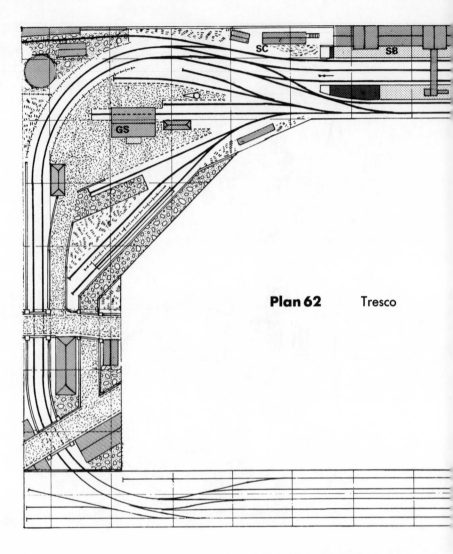

Plan 62   Tresco

Plan No. 62   Tresco
OO gauge 4.50 m × 2.40 m; Open motive power;
Country of origin England; **Other recommended
gauges** HO, N; **Minimum radius** 600 mm; **Train
length** 6 coaches; Large points; Main line continuous run leaving room for car in garage.

Tresco represents the conventional round-the-
garage-wall approach. This type of layout is
really best where the garage is wider than the
2.4 m I have specified, but providing the
baseboards are supported on brackets with the

underside at least 1.5 m clear of the floor, most
modern cars will go underneath. A lift-out
section spans the doorway. I have suggested a
viaduct here since, providing the tracks are laid
on 6 mm ply with 50 × 25 mm timber piers
beneath the decorative masonry shell, a strong
yet light timber girder can be built which
supports a relatively light scenic section.

   Tresco is quite interesting because it is not a
true four-track station. The centre road is bi-
directional and intended largely for freight,
whilst the loop can act as a terminal road, the

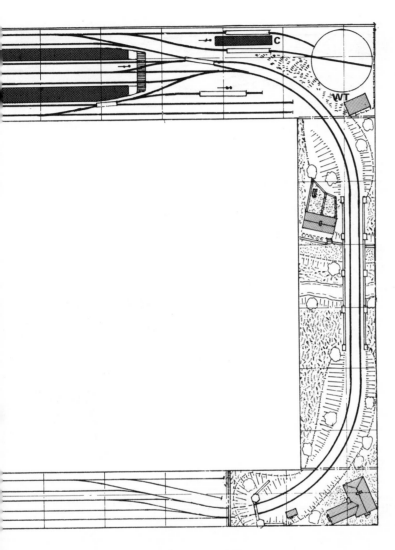

local services turning round in the central road of the storage loops. The goods yard is nicely spread out so that there appears to be room for lorries and carts to turn around between the tracks. The short spur nearest the main line is intended to house the brake van during re-marshalling. It is a fairly conventional scheme, but, as it is capable of handling reasonably long main line trains, a very satisfying one.

Of course, if the whole garage is available for the layout, so much the better. As an old friend pointed out, the car is made to stand out in the

rain, whereas the majority of model railways require a roof over their heads. If you can arrange a carport, or, best of all, convert to a double garage, so much the better. I know of one case where the garage was extended backwards and with the far end devoted to the layout and with loops laid around the car space, a very effective model capable of handling nine coach trains resulted. The following plans assume that one of these alternatives is followed, and that the entire space can be devoted to the layout.

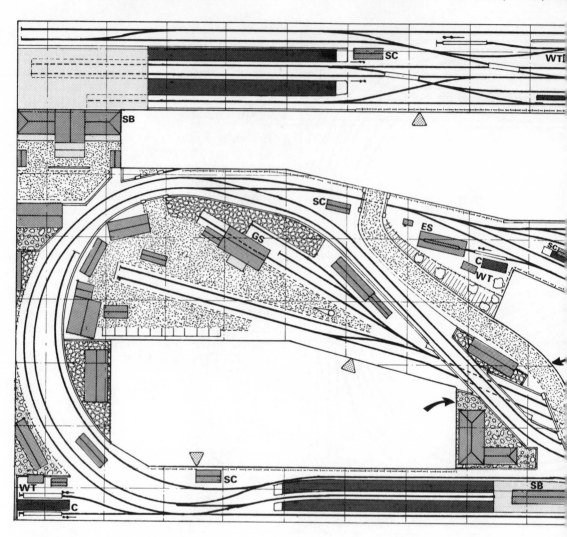

Plan 63   Applegate

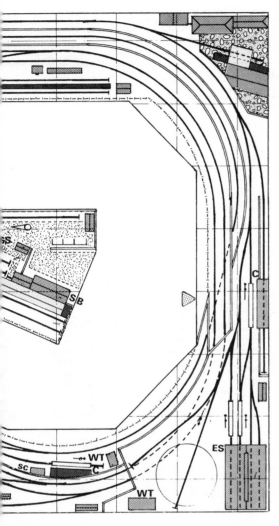

Plan No. 63 Applegate

EM gauge 4.80 m × 2.40 m; Steam motive power; **Country of origin** Britain; **Other recommended gauges** OO, HO, N*; **Minimum radius** 750 mm; **Train length** 5 coaches; Large points; Enlargement of *Maybank* occupying whole of standard garage.

Occasionally a plan takes charge and ends up looking rather different from my initial sketches. **Applegate** is a prime example of this. Originally I intended merely to open out the basic arrangement of Plan No. 44, **Banwell**, but by the time I had decided that a low-level goods yard would be fun and a main line reverse loop highly convenient it seemed a pity not to add a single track branch terminus as well. Then I threw in a couple of carriage sidings, complete with the narrow platform for the cleaners to get into every compartment. The through station collected a central bay for branch services and the result is an exciting scheme that really needs five operators to work the line fully, though one man could operate a skeleton service.

Plan 64
Sanditon

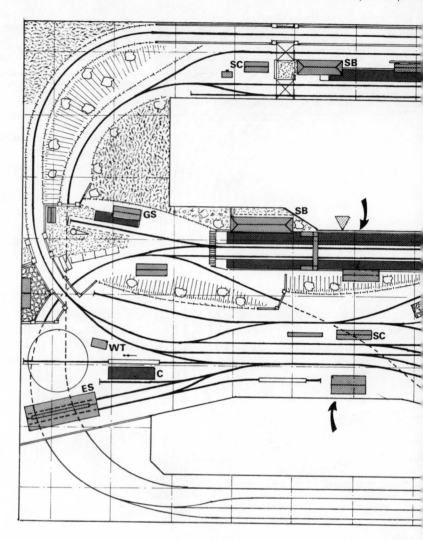

Plan No. 64 Sanditon
OO gauge 4.50 m × 2.40 m; Steam motive power; **Country of origin** Britain (Devon); **Other recommended gauges** HO, N*; **Minimum radius** 600 mm; **Train length** 4 coaches; Medium points; Branch line system in garage.

Plan No. 64 provides a branch line system, loosely based on the arrangement that existed between Sidmouth and Exmouth. **Sanditon** has little else in common with the prototype system, indeed it could prove rather difficult to work out a reasonable geographic map of the railway.

The main terminus on the high level depicts a station that grew over the years, the older section under the roof being supplemented by a slightly longer open platform with adjacent carriage sidings. This allows one to recreate the old summer Saturday services so characteristic of the West Country railways until the late 1950s. To cope with the weekend rush to and from the coast innumerable extra trains were run, with many services run in duplicate and triplicate. All resorts received at least one through service from London, often amounting to ten coaches. These trains, made up from older

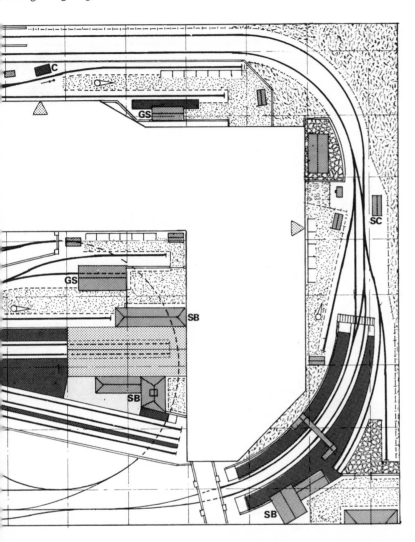

but serviceable main line stock, were often stabled at the termini during the week, or on spare sidings along the branches.

The two passing stations have very simple goods facilities, but this will allow one to operate a proper pick-up service, possibly using some form of way–bill operating system to add interest. The smaller terminus is long and thin, with the goods yard extending beyond the platforms, a not uncommon arrangement and rather useful where, as in this case, we have ample length and little width to spare. A rising track makes a continuous circuit, but the link between the reverse loop and the storage roads behind the main terminus is there to allow more prototypical reversal for serious operation.

The model can be operated single-handed, preferably with walkaround control rather than fixed operating positions. Naturally the points would be controlled from a local panel, which would also deal with track sectionalizing. Provision should also be made for multiple operator use, since running a system such as this with a group of friends is one of the more pleasant aspects of our hobby.

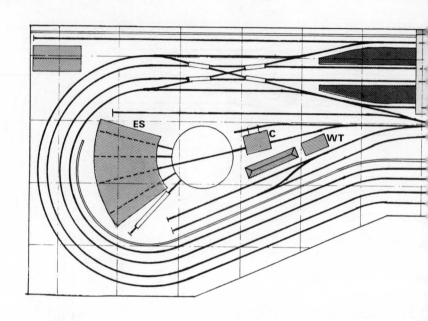

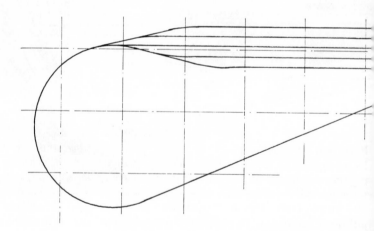

Plan 65   Strelsau

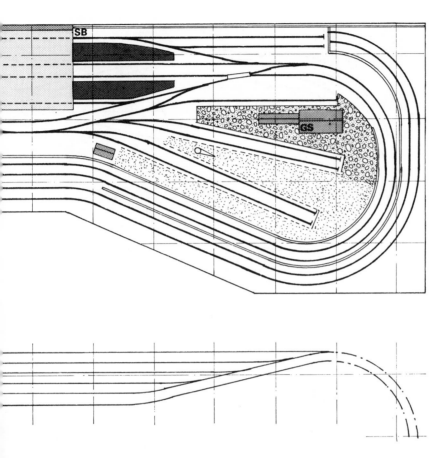

Plan No. 65 Strelsau

HO gauge 4.50 m × 1.35 m; Diesel motive power; **Country of origin** Ruritania; **Other recommended gauges** OO, N; **Minimum radius** 400 mm; **Train length** 7 coaches; Medium points; Continental layout based on Marklin design.

For Plan No. 65 we turn to the Continent for our inspiration. I have suggested Ruritania, for as Anthony Hope did no more than tell us that there was a railway serving **Strelsau** we can do much as we please, with operating practice following the DB at a respectful distance.

The track plan is a development of an arrangement used by Marklin on a couple of their demonstration layouts and is a very ingenious way of arranging a conventional oval scheme without making the operator stretch too far to reach the back. I have, however, added a low-level reverse loop under the main station to provide additional storage for trains, something that is not necessary for a trade demonstration but is almost essential on a large home-based model. **Strelsau** takes up one wall of the garage, and is a very impressive way of producing a highly developed 'train set oval' layout.

The scissors crossover with slip points is a very common arrangement on the Continent, but as there was an example of this compact formation at Ilfracombe this layout could be adapted to British practice with very little bother. I still cannot work out how to get to the goods yard with a lorry, but then, odd things do happen in Ruritania!

Plan 66
Tuxedo Junction

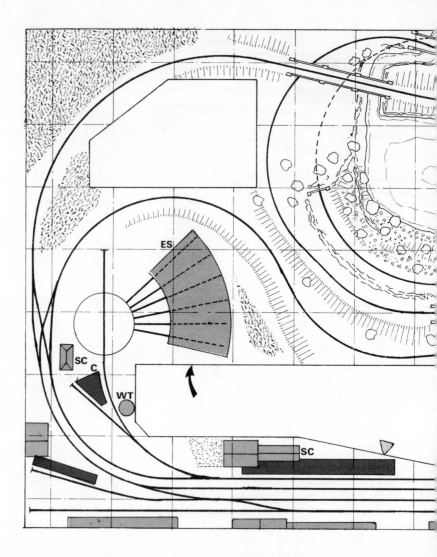

Plan No. 66 Tuxedo Junction

HO gauge 4.50 m × 2.40 m; Open motive power; **Country of origin** America; **Other recommended gauges** OO, N*; **Minimum radius** 600 mm; **Train length** 8 coaches; Large points; Dumbell (dogbone) scheme based on recent USA practice.

We are even further overseas with Plan No. 66, having crossed the Atlantic. I have only included two USA-style layouts because their operating practice differs radically from ours. In Europe,

when traffic increases we add extra trains; in the USA, they add more cars and build bigger locomotives. Added to this is the fact that although a boxcar is only 40 to 50 ft long, it is still much longer than the majority of European freight vehicles. In my opinion, you need plenty of room to model a USA prototype in HO, and a fair amount of space for N if you are to capture the spirit of the prototype. Even so, this model is still something of a compromise and only approximates to strict prototype practice.

The layout is the useful dumbell or, to use the

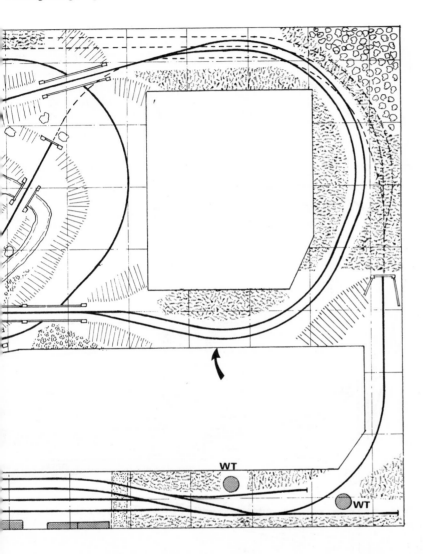

American term, dogbone, with reverse loops at each end, again a type of plan that requires ample room to be effective. I have introduced a spiral just to liven things up and looped it around a lake which is more than just a pretty addition to the scenery. The far tracks are rather inaccessible, but if the lake is made to hinge downwards, the shoreline making a clean edge to the resulting hole, easy maintenance access is provided.

The station layout is typical of USA single-track practice. The main line is that nearest the depot, the further tracks are sidings, where the inferior trains come off the main to allow the superior ones to pass. The rules of superiority are straightforward, but lengthy so I am not going to go into them here. The rear road is a team track, a line that serves a number of industries. In accordance with USA practice, the better part of town is in the operating well, the visible part is 'on the wrong side of the tracks'.

As, like most of my generation, I listen to Glen Miller recordings with fond nostalgia, what could I call this plan but **Tuxedo Junction**?

Plan No. 67   Laurenceton

OO gauge 4.50 m × 2.70 m; Open motive power; **Country of origin** Britain; **Other recommended gauges** HO, N*; **Minimum radius** 600 mm; **Train length** 8 coaches; Large points; Out-and-back system equally suited to Continental practice.

Plan No. 67 is the most ambitious of our garage schemes, and once again is designed primarily for intensive operation. Furthermore, on this occasion I have postulated a slightly wider site, since to swing a pair of double track loops from an island terminus requires at least 2.7 m in width. However, since in today's conditions a

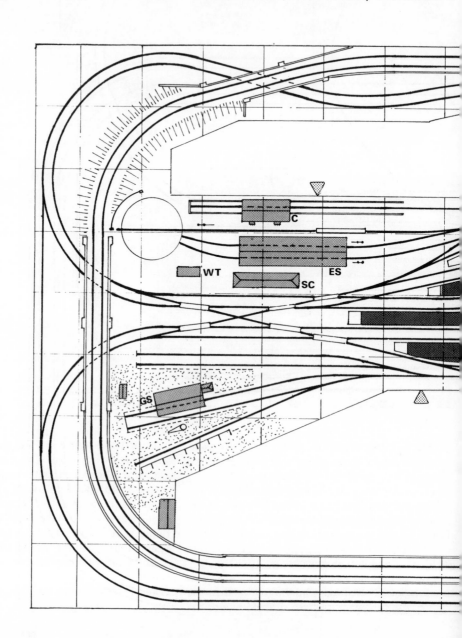

Plan 67
Laurenceton

layout of this nature would almost certainly be operated exclusively by ready-to-run stock, all of which is perfectly happy on 450 mm radius, it is possible to narrow the overall size, not at the expense of the operating wells, but of the spread of the only station.

Although conceived as a steam-age model, it would be easily adapted to diesel haulage by the simple process of eliminating the locomotive depot and replacing it with a few lie-by sidings. This layout is equally suited to European use, and will not require any alterations to the trackage, as you can operate it as left-hand or right-hand running with no further ado. Some of

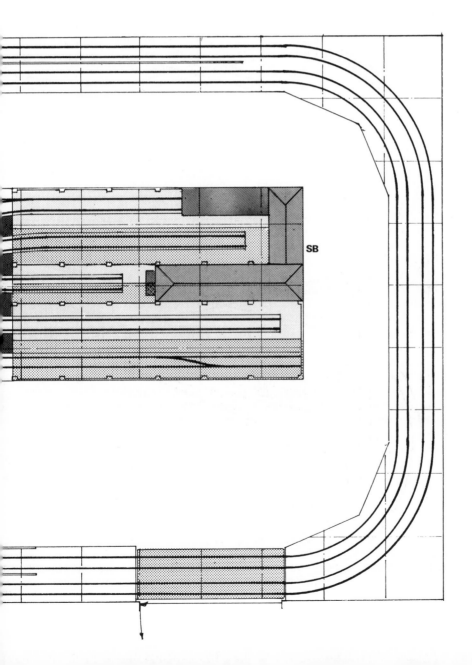

the buildings would need altering — the goods shed is typically British.

Laurenceton therefore comprises a straight-forward out-and-back circuit around the walls of the garage, with a central terminus. I have shown how the usual side access door would fit. The main garage doors will, of course, provide access to the tracks on the left, which in a conventional room would be almost completely inaccessible. There appears to be quadruple track, but we have simply taken the main line twice around the garage, thus ensuring a very long main line indeed. Some form of automatic block control would be very useful as you could then have around six trains lapping the circuit at any one time. Electrical enthusiasts can enjoy working out the circuits, or you can use one of the Continental systems, which are relatively easy to incorporate into a layout of this nature.

The terminus is the main feature of course, and my plan is intended to avoid any hint of symmetry in the track layout. Indeed, there are two smaller local platforms in the centre, though as the smallest will easily handle a four-coach train, it is not exactly short. The longest platforms will handle a full length HST if required.

The station buildings are moderately elaborate and the suggested overall roof is very complex, two large identical roofs linked by a shorter, smaller section. This would be a major modelling project and is the main reason why there is little scenic detail elsewhere on the model. As I see it, this building should be a magnificent, fully-detailed model based on any major prototype station you happen to like. It should be an eye-catcher, with the rest of the layout as a frame. Furthermore, the trains should be equally effective, for you will be able to run expresses that really do look like expresses.

Whilst timetable working of a sort is possible, the main interest will lie in working the main terminus. It is feasible to run the entire model single-handed from a control position close to the goods yard, but even with automatic block working on the main line, you will need two hands to reach something like the full capacity of the scheme, so a subsidiary board on the other side is suggested. The operator here would handle the locomotive shed and possibly his side of the terminus as well.

The layout, like many in this book, has been designed to use commercial track. This is why there is only a single-track link across the top of the 'Y'; a double junction using standard diamonds will simply not fit. Furthermore, unless you are extremely skilful do not make your own curved junctions. This type of formation is even more difficult to make than a double slip, and the distance from the operating edge will make a derailment even more bother than usual — and that is saying a lot.

The potential of a garage site in OO or HO is enormous, and I have done little more than scratch the surface of the subject. My plans are all for a minimum-sized structure, although most garages are slightly larger. There is some element of compromise inherent in all these plans. One would prefer larger radii and longer trains, but I think I have shown that the garage allows one to produce a really interesting model railway and certainly to reach as high a level of complexity as the majority of us are prepared to consider. When you combine this with the fact that the space is there, frequently under-used, it becomes the most obvious home for a serious model railway.

Before I leave the garage, the possibility of using it to house a semi-portable layout must be considered. The idea is to store the layout at the far end of the garage and erect it for short periods with the car standing outside. There are two snags, neither insuperable. The main one is that a garage floor generally slopes to provide drainage, so legs would have to be suitably adjusted, and there would be bother if the line were taken to an exhibition hall. The other is that with the vulnerable baseboards across the end wall, an incautious entry into the garage could have disastrous results. I advise a Dexion or Handy Angle supporting frame with a good stout central section to take the odd accidental knock. If the girders were faced with wood, you would do little damage to the car's bumpers either.

CHAPTER 13

Above it all

It certainly requires a good deal of outlay in time and money to turn a cold, cobwebby cock-loft into a cosy comfortable railway room, but where it is a practicable proposition one does get a very useful space indeed. There are only two main difficulties, the entry hatch and the header tanks which, both of which, by Murphy's Law, seem to be put in the most awkward place possible. Having said all that, there is generally so much spare room in the older type of loft that most of the preceding plans can be readily fitted in with only a little modification, whilst the fact that the hatch is inside the layout eliminates the need for a lift-out section across the doorway.

Unfortunately, with modern houses not only is the headroom more restricted, due to the lower slope, but the pre-fabricated roof trusses have crossbracing where one least wants it! However, providing you are prepared to accept certain limitations, these timbers can prove very useful. It is a case of going along with the existing structure rather than fighting it every bit of the way.

Plan No. 68   Loftberg
HOm gauge 4.20 m × 2.40 m; Electric motive power; **Country of origin** Switzerland; **Other recommended gauges** OOn3, HOn3; **Minimum radius** 350 mm; **Train length** 6 coaches; Medium points; Metre gauge system in modern loft based on RhB practice.

Take, for example, Plan No. 68 which once again is based on Swiss metre gauge practice, using those awkward timbers as foundations for the Alps. The little tinted areas at either edge on the plan indicate the line of the rafters. The centres are taken from my own loft and may not agree with yours.

Indeed, **Loftberg** is a very complex model and, should you decide that it is for you, I advise a very careful preliminary study. You could build a model of the layout to clarify the various levels in your mind, but my own preference would be for a card, string and wire lash-up on site, which will not only settle precisely how large everything is, but will let you see how best to hang or support the track bases and scenic features from the rafters.

The scheme incorporates a single junction station, with a small goods yard and a locomotive shed. There is a low level continuous run, which provides you with something to use whilst the main trackage is fitted in. This comprises one small and one long reverse loop, providing a good long run for your models, and is a development of the dumbell arrangement.

The main scenic feature is a gorge with a lot of bridges, located between a pair of roof principals. You have three options, the most ambitious of which is to select suitable designs from the prototype and model these as closely as you think fit. The second is to make good use of

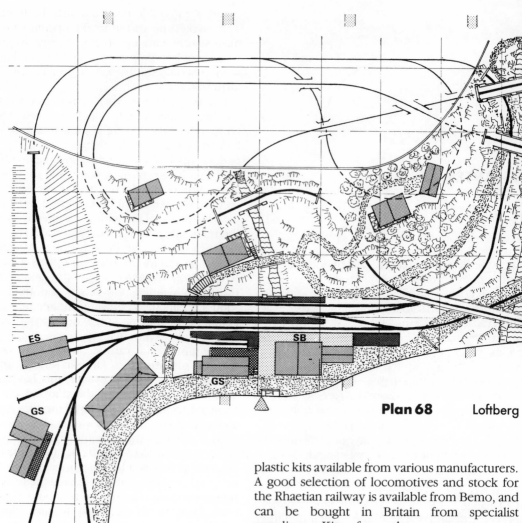

Plan 68   Loftberg

the many kits produced by Continental manufacturers. The third course is to make some and kit bash where you think fit. The low-level bridge in the front carries both road and rail, whilst the large one over the station throat is intended to be a steel girder pattern bridge.

The various buildings dotted around the layout are there just to add substance to the plan. In all probability you will use the excellent plastic kits available from various manufacturers. A good selection of locomotives and stock for the Rhaetian railway is available from Bemo, and can be bought in Britain from specialist suppliers. Kits for other prototypes are obtainable, and more metre gauge equipment is coming on to the market.

As the system uses overhead power supply, it is tempting to utilize this for current collection and so avoid any electrical complications with the two reverse loops. However, as there are kits for metre gauge steam locomotives, and as the RhB runs regular steam specials, you may in due course want to run one of these over the layout, or you might decide to have a model of a diesel tractor. My own suggestion would be to stick to two-rail traction, with provision for use of the overhead if required.

Plan No. 69 Grantchester
OO gauge 4.65 m × 3.15 m; Steam motive power; **Country of origin** Britain; **Other recommended gauges** EM, HO, N*; **Minimum radius** 600 mm; **Train length** 7 coaches; Large points; British main line scheme in modern loft.

Plan No. 69 also caters for the modern roof timbers, with the result that the overall width of the layout proper is relatively narrow. Indeed, the area is narrower than it appears, since the road that completely encircles **Grantchester** is set at a higher level, with those struts coming up underneath.

Fortunately, there is just about enough usable width behind the timbers to allow a 600 mm radius curve so that a set of hidden loops on the

otherwise invisible main line may be fitted in. They would be visible to the operator on the main station, and are of ample length to give a considerable degree of tolerance in spotting the train. It would still be best to arrange for some form of train detection.

I have gone into this earlier, but there is another arrangement which is well worth considering where there is some tolerance on a hidden siding. A high-resistance relay that will operate on 12V DC is wired in series with the feed to a length of track some 300 to 400 mm long. When the locomotive runs onto this section, the relay will be energized, whilst the high resistance of the wiring will effectively stop the train, albeit as if it had hit a wall. The relay can then energize an indicator on a descriptive panel. To restart the train you press a button wired across the relay. This shorts out the high resistance winding and starts the train, but should additionally, through further relays, set up the exit road or you will derail it almost immediately afterwards.

The same result can be obtained by simply wiring a miniature 12V lamp in series with the feed to this section. However, this has only a limited application, since the relay can also be arranged to protect the rear of the halted train and switch out the track circuit. For this you need a latching relay circuit. In other words, when you complete the circuit one of the relay contacts is arranged to pass current to the relay coil, and until this circuit is cleared the relay will remain held on. The release pushbutton would need to work another relay to carry out the number of switching circuits needed. An alternative would be a British Telecom pattern key switch, which has a number of contacts.

A further refinement is to use a simple transistor circuit to detect and amplify the operating current. This obviates the need to find a relay that will work on less than 12V DC. I admit that this is only a very sketchy description, but then this is not a manual on model railway electrification.

So much for the electrics! The main station is quite an impressive affair, with four main platforms which can handle a seven-coach train with ease. There is just room for a seven-coach

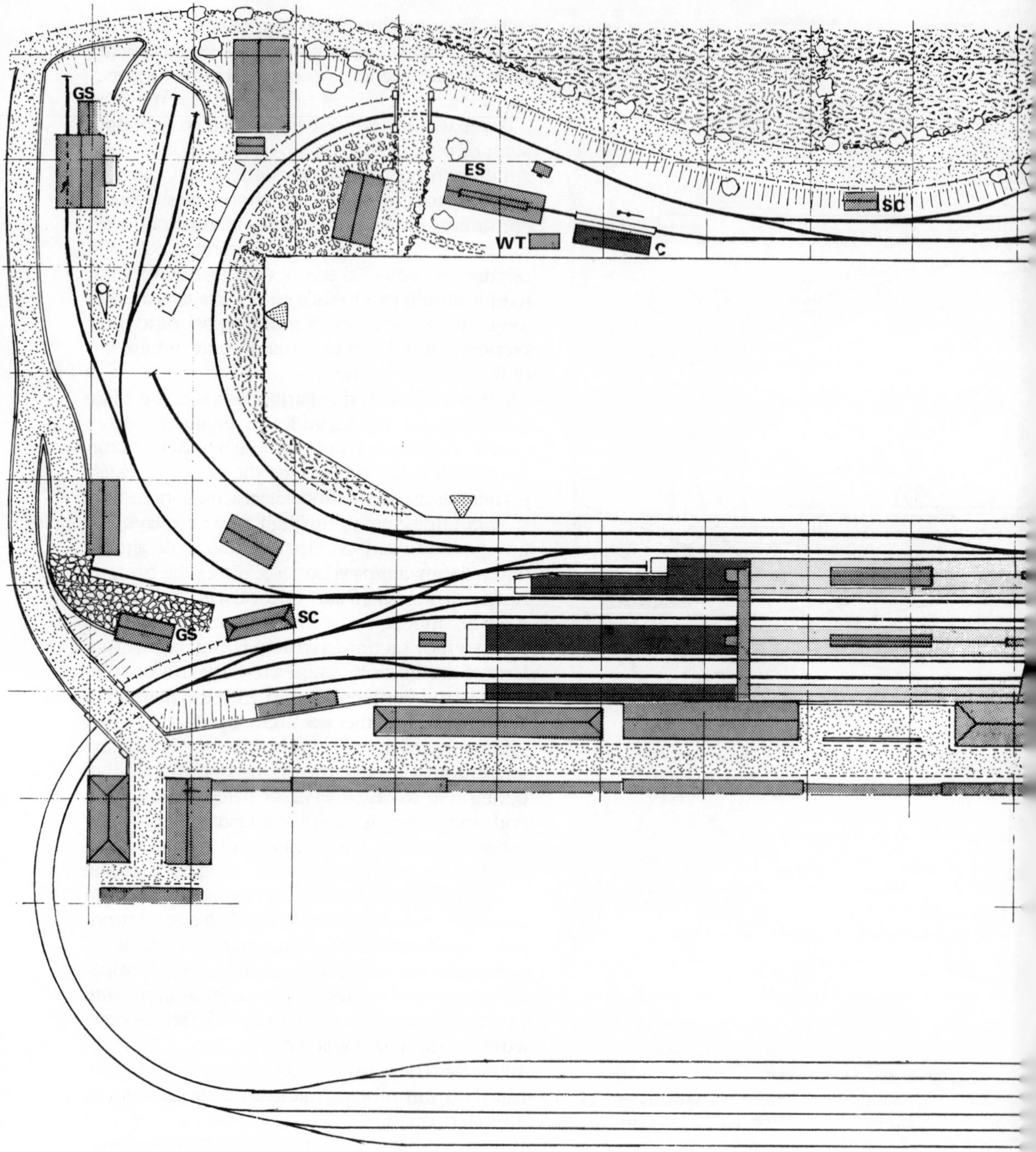

GS

ES

SC

WT

C

SC

GS

SC

GS

Plan 69   Grantchester

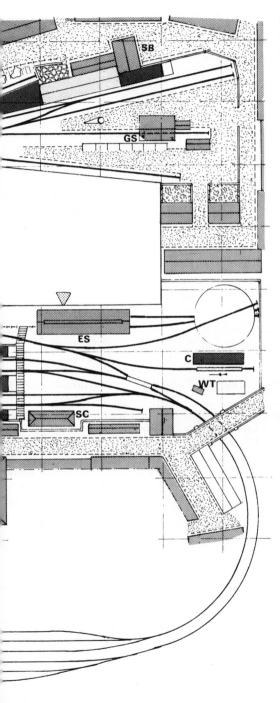

HST, though somehow I cannot reconcile modern Inter-City running with a steam-age single track branch. You are free to please yourself.

The station is arranged to permit reversal in either direction on the main line, and a small but comprehensive motive power depot allows one to turn tender locomotives when this is done. I am rather pleased with the arrangement of pointwork at each end, giving reasonable access to the various roads without being so complicated it cannot be built up from standard commercial turnouts. Scratchbuilt pointwork would be very nice, providing you can make it with sufficient accuracy.

The goods yard is possibly a little too small for so imposing a station, so let us assume that the main goods traffic takes place somewhere along the main line beyond one of the two bridges.

The branch line platform is much shorter, part of it being taken up with a safety spur used during shunting movements. Although a direct exit to the main line is possible under the bridge, this is not strictly in accordance with prototype practice, since it would involve running through the locomotive yard, which is not really the done thing. In any case, I envisage the branch being worked in connection with the main line trains, with no direct through running.

The branch terminus layout is fairly conventional apart from one feature, the locomotive release crossover halfway along the platform. This particular arrangement was very common, and as it adds an extra siding to the yard it is fine when as in this case we have ample room for the station. It is interesting to note that although the branch station is much simpler and only accommodates a four-coach train, it is nearly as long as the main line station. Neither station is based on any particular prototype, but the basic features are prototypical. The scenic setting is more imaginative.

The road behind the main station would be at least 100 mm above track level to give good clearance on the rafters. This means that the massive bridge spanning the platforms can have the main girders below the roadway, a more common arrangement. There is a reasonably large station building, with a small bus station alongside. Further along, another set of buildings handles the parcels traffic and is linked to the platforms by means of a bridge with goods lifts.

Instead of a backscene proper, I have suggested low relief buildings with three streets running off, the view being blocked by a further set of buildings behind. This could be fairly simple, with card cut-out buildings or a piece of sustained miniature architecture. One would probably begin with card buildings for speed and make the superior models later on, a pleasant project to keep one happy for years. The branch has fewer buildings shown around the station, but there is nothing to stop you from building a small town on a hillside, rising in terraced ranks until it reaches the roof.

If you are ambitious, then it would be perfectly possible to build a working tram layout through the town. The only thing that stopped me suggesting this was the feeling that there was quite enough to be getting along with already. However, if this were a syndicate scheme then this objection would no longer apply; all you would need is a tramway fanatic in the group.

The main station has an east and west pair of signal boxes. If this particular model were to be built, the owner would soon find out why this was done so frequently on the prototype. I have shown four operating positions, which would be advisable for maximum train density. It would also make it much easier to form a syndicate to build and maintain the model. There is also the point that with timbers crossing over the operating well, it would be best for each operator to stay put during a running session.

It is worth mentioning that whilst the modern prefabricated loft is narrow it is usually fairly long, since it is impracticable to make up a hipped roof with factory-built framing, except at a prohibitive cost. The loft I had in mind, one over a house I once owned, was a good 2 m longer, and with this particular arrangement would have allowed ten-coach trains.

There is one definite snag, the water tanks and their associated header pipes, which is why the branch swings out. The tank, one hopes, would go nicely behind the scenery, under a modelled hillside.

Plan No. 70 Nelson (Block Plan)
EM gauge 6.10 m × 4.10 m; Steam motive power; **Country of origin** Britain; **Other recommended gauges** OO, HO, N; **Minimum radius** 750 mm; **Train length** 9 coaches; Large points; Block plan of diorama scheme, showing relative location of units.

Finally, in Plan No. 70 we look at the case of the really large loft, the sort of thing one finds over a pre-war three bedroom bungalow. The idea stems from some excellent work done by my old friend Jack Nelson in his loft, with sections of the LNWR arranged as dioramas. **Nelson** is more conventional, with five separate layout units arranged around a central hobbies room. These are linked by hidden corners so that although moderately sharp curves are employed they are completely out of sight. You will see that I have shown a large workbench and added a dressmaker's dummy, since the room is equally suited to home dressmaking. Indeed, with the addition of a colour television set and some provision for making hot drinks it is quite likely that everyone would spend more time up here than in the official living room, and the cost of fitting out the loft would be more than justified.

Plan No. 70a Nelson
EM gauge 4.50 m × 0.75 m; Steam motive power; **Country of origin** Britain; **Other recommended gauges** OO, HO, N; **Minimum radius** 1,000 mm; **Train length** 9 coaches; Large points; Main through station for diorama layout.

The main station is a large four-track affair with

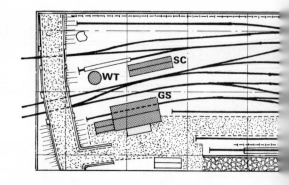

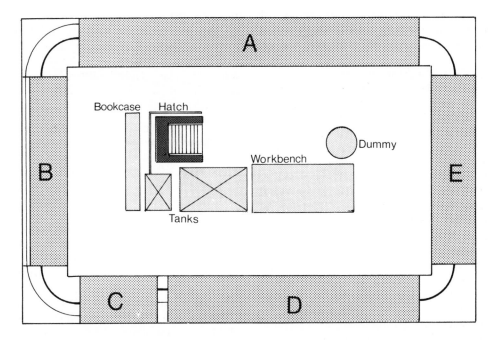

Plan 70   Nelson (Block Plan)

ample goods facilities and a branch bay that only looks small by comparison with the main line, where nine coaches can be readily accommodated. There are a couple of locomotive spurs at the right-hand end, whilst the goods yard is of reasonable size. It is just the sheer size of the layout that deceives.

Plan No. 70b   Weston North
EM gauge 2.40 m × 0.53 m; Steam motive power; **Country of origin** Britain; **Other recommended gauges** OO, HO, N; **Minimum radius** None; **Train length** 9 coaches; No points; Scenic feature, comprising the platforms and structures only.

Plan 70a   Nelson

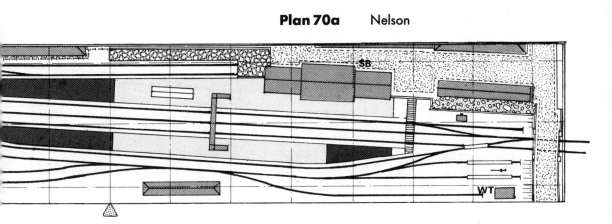

Plan No. 70b, **Weston North**, is a purely scenic feature, a normal double-track through station, fully detailed and provided with two dummy sidings. These, whilst apparantly useless, would be the home for all those vehicles which will not run reliably without the attention you honestly intend giving them someday — when there isn't something more interesting to do.

Plan No. 70c   Canal Bridge
EM gauge 1.00 m × 0.60 m; Steam motive power; **Country of origin** Britain; **Other recommended gauges** OO, HO, N; **Minimum radius** 1,000 mm; **Train length** 9 coaches; No points; Scenic diorama for larger layout.

The single track which ran behind the backscene appears at high level in Plan No. 70c where rail and canal intertwine. Note how the gaps in the backscene for the tracks are hidden behind buildings or in a small thicket of trees. Nothing much happens here, it is just a piece of pretty scenic modelling and, providing you really concentrate on your craftsmanship, is quite likely to be the main focus of attention of any lay visitors, particularly if you include the pub that's frequently found near a canal lock. I wonder why?

Plan No. 70d   Payne
EM gauge 4.50 m × 0.60 m; Steam motive power; **Country of origin** Britain; **Other recommended gauges** OO, HO, N; **Minimum radius** 1,000 mm; **Train length** 5 coaches; Large points; Country terminus for diorama layout with storage roads underneath.

Plan No. 70d is a fairly large country terminus

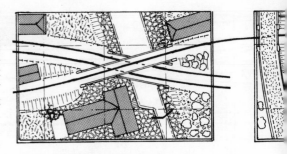

Plan 70c   Canal Bridge

with a very convenient track plan. There are two run-round loops at **Payne**, one for the passenger traffic, the other for goods, whilst a small locomotive shed caters for the branch tank engine. The main platform will comfortably house a four-coach train, but could be extended to take five if you liked to relocate the signal cabin.

Plan No. 70e   Nelson MPD
EM gauge 2.40 m × 0.60 m; Steam motive power; **Country of origin** Britain; **Other recommended gauges** OO, HO, N; **Minimum radius** 1,000 mm; **Train length** 9 coaches; Large points; Steam motive power depot for diorama layout.

The final unit is a small motive power depot for **Nelson**, capable of holding eight large locomotives under cover. As space is not restricted too badly, we have a loop road around the coaling stage, so that one locomotive can leave the turntable whilst a second is busy

Plan 70b   Weston North

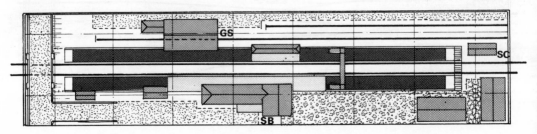

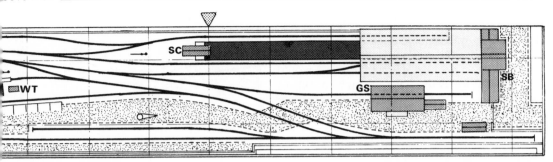

Ian 70d   Payne

replenishing its tender. Alternatively, if only the first 100 mm or so of the locomotive shed were modelled, suggesting that the rest extended beyond the confines of the diorama, all locomotives could stand in the open, implying a much larger MPD.

There's a small factory siding included as a suggestion for filling up a corner, but the main interest here is the locomotive depot. Which brings me to a simple idea for those who do not have a large loft or similar area available and for locomotive modellers who have not yet begun to build their layout. A thoroughgoing locomotive depot does not take up much space and provides a good test ground for newly-built models. There are now a large number of books around providing ample details of prototype sheds, and although most are much too big for a scale model, there are a number of compact designs that can be squeezed into a small space.

In such a case, however, I would be inclined to model the front of the shed only, with ample standing room in the open.

I would suggest that the fascias around the dioramas were made from plastic coated ply, with a wood grain effect. Below the layout would be bookshelves, cupboards and strategically located entries to get beneath and behind the baseboards for maintenance. This would be cramped, but not unworkable.

As an added refinement, you could fit lightweight plastic windows in front of the dioramas. I have seen such materials sold in DIY stores as secondary double glazing and I have no doubt that they would add considerably to the appearance of the model. The glazing on the operable sections could be arranged to slide sideways for operator access, but on the purely scenic areas it could be a semi-permanent fixture.

Plan 70e   Nelson MPD

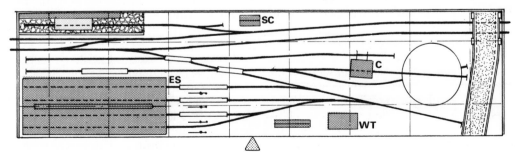

CHAPTER 14
Setting it out

Although the schemes in this book appear to be highly finished, they are no more than project plans put forward as a starting point. They were all designed loosely, in other words, I have slightly over-estimated the size of turnouts and other fixed features, allowed for generous clearances on gradients and so ensured that the proposed layout will drop easily into the quoted area. Or, as is more than likely, there is a small degree of tolerance to allow for individual variations during construction. As a result, I have not shown track centres, nor have I indicated the toe of the points. Do not scale off a drawing; this is a fundamental rule of workshop practice.

In this instance it would be doubly misleading, since the plans were produced to a scale of 1:12, while the tracks were drawn with an 0.8 mm stylus and are therefore 9.6 mm wide! In other words, they represent broad flowing slashes made by a thick felt-tipped pen. When drawing out a plan to full size, my construction lines are no more than half a millimetre in width.

Let us go a little further. A detailed working drawing should be:

a) Fully dimensioned

b) Produced from detailed calculations.

Leaving aside the work involved in such a chore, a serious objection remains. To calculate a track plan in full detail, the exact type and make of points must be specified. This is clearly undesirable, except in a book sponsored by a track manufacturer and clearly stating that it is solely for X's track. For this book, I assume that you will decide which manufacturer's track you want to use.

In any case, a detailed working drawing is not necessary. A model railway is a one-off project and so it is best to lay it out full size, either on the baseboard, or better still, on large sheets of inexpensive paper. At the same time, you should check train lengths by the simple business of assembling from your collection the sort of train you want to use on the model. Then and only then can you be sure the size is correct. There is nothing more infuriating than discovering after the tracks are in place that a small adjustment could have provided room for an additional coach, or, worse still, that your main run-round loop is 10 mm too short to allow you to get round the train you intended to run.

It may well be that you have found a plan that not only fits your space, but also appears to meet all your requirements. More probably, you will have a slightly different site and would prefer a different station arrangement. You may want to work in a different scale. What then? You change the design!

Unless the changes are relatively minor, you would be well advised to produce another layout plan, in which case do not be misled by my drawings. You do not need to be anywhere near so detailed. You can block in a lot of the lineside features or simply write over the area 'shops', 'rough ground with trees' or whatever.

else takes your fancy.

It is always possible to stretch a plan to fit a larger site but you can only reduce the size of a plan by:

a) Reducing the length of trains
b) Reducing the track radius
c) Reducing the number of sidings.

Even when there is scope for doing so, you are unlikely to save very much on the designed plan. Let us look a little further into this.

You have four basic parameters which set the size of your model. Of these only one is rigid, the size of point formations. The next parameter is the length of the longest train, and whilst you can make adjustments, reductions are generally done reluctantly.

These two sizes are best determined with the actual items involved, for although pointwork sizes can be determined with reasonable accuracy at full size, it is very easy to misalign paper plans. Do check the alignment of the rails across the joins with scrupulous care since badly aligned pointwork completely ruins running.

Track radii can be manipulated to a fair degree, and gradients can be slightly steepened. I do not, however, recommend any significant reduction, merely a 10 per cent skimming at the most.

As I said at the outset, the grid is 300 mm square for the gauge quoted. If you prefer imperial standard, then the grid should be taken as one foot square. For other scales the following conversions apply:

	Metric	Imperial
O gauge	525 mm	21 in
S gauge	356 mm	14.25 in
TT gauge	225 mm	9 in
N gauge	150 mm	6 in

NOTE This does not apply to Plans 22 to 26

I must again emphasize that only the track lines are at all fixed. All the buildings and scenic details are just my idea of what would look pleasing. In addition, I have tried to make each scenic treatment different in some respect, so you may well find that the arrangement of buildings on a track layout you do not particularly like will fit into the scheme you prefer. Do swap items about to suit your idea of a layout. As I have tried to make plain, these schemes are only the starting point for your unique model railway.

Railway buildings

I have only identified those buildings closely associated with the railway proper, since these are the essential features. As the ground plans are, to a reasonable degree, interchangeable, I would like to add a few general observations.

Station building

This is a rather loose term embracing the main offices on a station. In practice, you will often find waiting rooms, shelters, refreshment rooms etc separate from the main buildings. There will probably be a small shed for servicing the oil lamps which were standard fittings on most semaphore signals and needed to be cleaned, refilled and have their wicks changed at regular intervals.

Signal cabin

The signal cabin not only controls the points and signals, but it also contains the block telegraph to communicate with adjacent sections. In the days before colour lights, a full station *always* had a signal box.

Halts were platforms without full signalling, and any points were controlled by ground frames. These were low-level lever frames, with a locking device to prevent unauthorized use, which might be housed in a small building looking like a miniature signal box. Ground frame boxes did not contain block telegraphs, but usually had a telephone in later years. (This is not a treatise on signalling; the above notes are no more than a rough guide to a very complex subject.)

Goods yards

Except at very small halts, some form of goods shed was provided so that items received could be safely stored until the consignee called or the railway carrier could deliver. For convenience, a raised loading platform was provided, and in many cases a large shed was built over the track. A crane would often be found inside. Usually, there was a spur track beyond the shed so that wagons could be pushed through and new ones take their place. This movement was usually carried out by horsepower, but on large yards, powered capstans were provided.

In addition to any crane inside the goods shed, a yard crane was usually provided to lift large loads off wagons. End loading docks for carriage and implement wagons (a precursor of the modern car carrier) were provided, as were loading docks for cattle and sheep.

Coal was always a vital part of railway traffic, and coal bins or coal drops were provided at most stations. These would be used by local coal merchants, who had an office alongside. In addition, many stations had a builders' yard where timber, bricks and cement were brought in by rail and distributed by horse and cart or lorry.

Locomotive facilities

The steam locomotive required copious draughts of water, hence large water tanks delivered hundreds of gallons a minute through large bore pipes to the water columns or cranes. There could also be coaling stages, ranging from a simple platform, a platform with crane, a raised ramp and the complex overtrack coal hoppers. In addition, pits were provided not only to receive ashes from the fires, but also to permit access to the internal machinery for oiling and maintenance.

The engine shed was the least important part of the complex, and although locomotives were stabled there overnight, its other purpose was a covered, and to a certain extent, weatherproof place where the fitters could carry out the routine adjustments needed to keep the locomotives working.

Drawing your own

First and foremost, although I own a battery of high-class drawing instruments and all the latest graphic aids to produce plans, I only used a small selection producing these plans. My principal tool was a good A3 drawing board, backed by a large bow compass. A selection of set squares, including some 'CJF specials' for 12°, 15° and 22.5° were also used along with the standard 45° and 30° squares. A couple of french curves

were employed to fair in curves. I also used a battery of four stylus pens. You will not need this much because my first plans were produced in cheap drawing books on a table, using a school ruler and a pair of school compasses.

Only a few of the plans were not preceded by at least one pencil rough, and these were developments of earlier schemes I had drawn out before. In over half the cases, I wished I could have produced further variants. Only the publisher's deadlines stopped me. So when you are preparing plans for your own personal pleasure do, please, explore all obvious variants in as much detail as you can.

Use good quality paper for the final plans, and do not expect to get more than a few small detailed jottings onto the traditional 'back of an envelope'. I find that anything smaller than A4 is terribly restrictive, and when I first began serious layout planning, I used large sheets of cartridge paper. A3 is adequate, but A2 is a better size for detailed track planning. In fact with plans, the bigger, the better.

Unless the drawing is intended for reproduction, there is no real need to ink it in. I prefer, for my own pleasure, to use pencil. The modern stylus propelling pencils make drawing a real delight, and with very little effort you can introduce some pleasing textures that are very difficult to approach in ink. If you want to pretty up a personal plan, then coloured pens are ideal.

I have used Letraset on the drawings, but I prefer, for my own pleasure, to hand-letter. If you find this difficult (it takes a good deal of practice to produce neat script) it is better to employ a cheap stencil, there are some excellent versions on the market nowadays. As you develop you will probably invest in more instruments, and there are some lovely items to be found in better stores.

Finally, do not expect to produce top quality plans at your first attempt. It took me some twenty years to develop a good style, and whilst you can save time by cribbing some of my ideas expect to spend a long time developing your own individual techniques. But always remember, the plan is only the first step, no matter how detailed you make it. It is nothing until you build the model.